Carb Cycling Air Fryer Cookbook

1200 Days Easy, Delicious and Quick Recipes for Sustainable
Healthy Eating and Increasing Energy

Stameria Racia

Table of Contents

INTRODUCTION

What is Carb Cycling?

Carb cycling involves going back and forth between high-carb days and low-carb days. There may even be "no-carb" days. You would usually have a high-carb day when you plan on exercising hard. On those days, your body needs more fuel, so you might eat 2 to 2.5 grams of carbs for every pound of your body weight.

The Principle of Carb Cycling

- Cycling between high, low, and moderate-carb days: Carb cycling involves alternating between days with higher carbohydrate intake (high-carb days), days with lower carbohydrate intake (low-carb days), and days with a moderate carbohydrate intake (moderate-carb days).

- Timing carbohydrate intake around activity levels: The distribution of high, low, and moderate-carb days can be based on your activity levels. High-carb days are often scheduled on days with intense workouts or physical activities that require increased energy. Low-carb days may be scheduled on rest days or days with light physical activity. Moderate-carb days can be scheduled on days with moderate exercise or training.

- Adjusting macronutrient intake: Along with varying carbohydrate intake, individuals may also adjust their fat and protein intake accordingly. While carbohydrate intake is manipulated, it's important to maintain adequate protein intake to support muscle maintenance and repair.

- Individualization: The structure and duration of carb cycling can vary based on individual goals, body composition, activity levels, metabolic factors, and personal preferences. It's important to tailor the approach to meet your specific needs and consult with a healthcare professional or registered dietitian for personalized guidance.

- Tracking and monitoring: Keeping track of your carbohydrate intake, as well as other macronutrients, can be helpful in implementing carb cycling effectively. This can be done through food diaries, tracking apps, or working with a nutritionist to ensure you're meeting your macronutrient goals.

- Adjusting based on feedback: It's important to listen to your body and adjust your carb cycling approach based on how you feel and the results you're experiencing. Monitoring factors such as energy levels, performance, body composition changes, and overall well-being can help you make necessary adjustments to optimize the approach.

Benefits of Carb Cycling

Carb cycling offers several potential benefits. Here are some of the key advantages associated with this dietary approach:

- Fat loss: Carb cycling can be an effective strategy for promoting fat loss. By cycling between low-carb and high-carb days, the body can utilize stored

fat as an energy source during low-carb days while replenishing glycogen stores on high-carb days. This can create a calorie deficit, leading to weight loss and improved body composition.

- Muscle preservation: When following a calorie-restricted diet for fat loss, there is a risk of losing muscle mass along with fat. By incorporating high-carb days into the plan, carb cycling can help preserve muscle glycogen stores, supporting muscle recovery and minimizing muscle breakdown.

- Enhanced athletic performance: Carbohydrates are the body's primary source of energy for high-intensity exercise. By strategically timing high-carb days around intense workouts or competitions, carb cycling can provide the necessary glycogen stores to fuel performance, improving endurance and power output.

- Improved metabolic flexibility: Consistently consuming a high-carbohydrate diet can lead to a reliance on carbohydrates as the primary fuel source. Carb cycling encourages the body to become more metabolically flexible by switching between carbohydrate and fat metabolism. This adaptability can enhance overall metabolic health.

- Hormonal regulation: Carbohydrate intake influences the production and release of various hormones, including insulin, leptin, and ghrelin. Carb cycling can help regulate these hormones, optimizing metabolism, hunger, satiety, and energy balance.

- Flexibility and sustainability: One of the benefits of carb cycling is its flexibility compared to strict, low-carb diets. It allows for the inclusion of higher-carb meals or days, which can make the diet more enjoyable and easier to stick to in the long term. This flexibility can improve adherence and overall dietary sustainability.

- Psychological benefits: Carb cycling can provide psychological relief for individuals who struggle with the strictness of conventional diets. Having structured high-carb days can help alleviate cravings, reduce feelings of deprivation, and promote a healthier relationship with food.

- Muscle fullness and vascularity: On high-carb days, glycogen replenishment can lead to increased muscle fullness and vascularity, giving a more visually appealing appearance.

It's worth noting that the specific benefits of carb cycling can vary among individuals, depending on factors such as activity levels, metabolic rate, body composition, and overall health. Additionally, it's important to tailor the approach to individual goals and preferences, seeking guidance from a healthcare professional or registered dietitian for personalized advice.

How Does Carb cycling Work?

Here's how carb cycling typically works:

- High-carb days: On high-carb days, you consume a higher amount of carbohydrates, usually around 50-60% of your total calorie intake. These days are intended to replenish glycogen stores, provide energy, and support intense physical activity. High-carb days are often scheduled on workout days to enhance performance and recovery.

- Low-carb days: On low-carb days, you consume fewer carbohydrates, typically around 10-30% of your total calorie intake. The focus is on consuming more protein, healthy fats, and non-starchy vegetables. The reduced carbohydrate intake helps lower insulin levels, which encourages the body to use stored fat as an energy source.

- Moderate-carb days: Some carb cycling plans incorporate moderate-carb days that fall between high and low-carb days. The carbohydrate intake on these days is usually around 30-50% of your total calorie intake. Moderate-carb days can provide a balance between energy and fat burning.

- The frequency of cycling can vary depending on individual goals and preferences. Some people follow a daily carb cycling approach, while others cycle on a weekly basis. For example, a common weekly cycle could be high-carb, low-carb, moderate-carb, low-carb, repeated throughout the week.

How to Use Air Fryer Correctly?

Using an air fryer correctly involves a few key steps and considerations to ensure optimal cooking results. Here's a guide to help you use an air fryer effectively:

- Read the manual: Start by thoroughly reading the instruction manual that comes with your specific air fryer model. It will provide important information about the features, functions, and safety precautions specific to your device.

- Preheat the air fryer: Most air fryers require preheating before use. Preheating helps create a hot cooking environment and ensures even cooking throughout the food. Set the air fryer to the recommended preheating temperature and allow it to heat up for a few minutes before adding the food.

- Choose the right cooking temperature: Air fryers typically have a wide temperature range, usually between 180°C (360°F) and 200°C (400°F). Refer to the recipe or cooking guidelines for the recommended temperature. If a recipe doesn't provide specific instructions, start with a temperature of 190°C (375°F) and adjust as needed.

- Use the right amount of oil: One of the advantages of an air fryer is that it requires less oil compared to traditional frying methods. Use a small amount of oil (usually 1-2 tablespoons) or cooking spray to lightly coat the food, helping to achieve a crispy texture. It's important not to use too much oil as it can cause the food to become greasy or create excessive smoke.

- Arrange food in a single layer: To ensure even cooking and proper air circulation, arrange the food in a single layer in the air fryer basket or tray. Overcrowding the basket can lead to uneven cooking and result in less crispy outcomes. If necessary, cook food in batches to maintain the single layer arrangement.

- Flip or shake the food: For even browning, flip or shake the food halfway through the cooking process. This helps ensure that all sides of the food are exposed to the hot air, resulting in more evenly cooked and crispy results.

- Adjust cooking time: Cooking times may vary depending on the type and quantity of food you are preparing. Follow the recommended cooking time provided in the recipe or cooking guidelines as a starting point. It's a good practice to check the food's doneness a few minutes before the recommended time and adjust accordingly.

- Monitor the cooking process: Keep an eye on the cooking process through the air fryer's transparent lid or by periodically opening the device. This allows you to check the progress, adjust temperature or time if needed, and prevent overcooking.

- Clean the air fryer properly: After each use, allow the air fryer to cool down completely before cleaning. Remove the basket or tray and wash it with warm, soapy water. Some air fryer components are dishwasher-safe, but always refer to the manual for specific cleaning instructions. Wipe the interior and exterior of the air fryer with a damp cloth or sponge.

- Experiment and practice: Every air fryer model is different, and it may take some trial and error to find the perfect cooking times and temperatures for your favorite recipes. Experiment with different settings, cooking times, and ingredients to get familiar with your air fryer's capabilities and achieve the desired results.

Remember to follow safety guidelines, such as placing the air fryer on a heat-resistant surface, keeping it away from flammable materials, and avoiding contact with water while operating. By following these steps and guidelines, you can make the most of your air fryer and enjoy delicious, crispy meals with less oil.

Chapter 1: Breakfast

Air Fryer Almond-Cinnamon Donuts

Prep Time: 15 Minutes
Cook Time: 30 Minutes
Serves: 12

Ingredients:

- 2 cups of almond flour
- 1 egg at room temperature
- ½ teaspoon of pure vanilla extract (no alcohol)
- ½ cup of stevia granulated sweetener
- 1 teaspoon of cinnamon
- Tbsp of apple cider vinegar
- 2 tablespoons of almond milk
- 2 tablespoons of lard softened
- Pinch of salt

Directions:

1. IAdd all ingredients into your food processor; process until a smooth dough is achieved.
2. ILine a baking sheet with baking paper.
3. IRoll dough out on a floured surface to ⅓ inch thickness.
4. ICut into doughnuts using a donut cutter.
5. IPlace donuts into the prepared baking sheet and let stand for about 15 minutes.
6. IPlace 4 donuts in a single layer in the air fryer (they should not be touching).
7. IClose the air fryer and set the temperature to 350 F.
8. ICook for about 5 to 6 minutes total (flip halfway through).
9. IRepeat with the remaining donuts.
10. ITransfer donuts to the serving plate.
11. ISprinkle with stevia sweetener and cinnamon, serve and enjoy!

Nutritional Value (Amount per Serving):

Calories: 34; Fat: 3.12; Carb: 1.62; Protein: 0.88

Air-Fryer Scallops

Prep Time: 20 Minutes
Cook Time: 20 Minutes
Serves: 2

Ingredients:

- 8 large (1-oz.) sea scallops, cleaned and patted very dry
- ¼ teaspoon ground pepper
- ⅛ teaspoon salt
- Cooking spray
- ¼ cup extra-virgin olive oil
- 2 tablespoons very finely chopped flat-leaf parsley
- 2 teaspoons very finely chopped capers
- 1 teaspoon finely grated lemon zest
- ½ teaspoon finely chopped garlic

Directions:

1. ISprinkle scallops with pepper and salt. Coat the basket of an air fryer with cooking spray. Place scallops in the basket and coat them with cooking spray. Place the basket in the fryer. Cook the scallops at 400°F until they reach an internal temperature of 120°F, about 6 minutes.
2. ICombine oil, parsley, capers, lemon zest and garlic in a small bowl. Drizzle over the scallops.

Nutritional Value (Amount per Serving):

Calories: 239; Fat: 12.7; Carb: 7.91; Protein: 24.12

Air Fryer Keto Breakfast Soufflé

Prep Time: 10 Minutes
Cook Time: 10 Minutes
Serves: 4

Ingredients:

- 8 large eggs, free-range or organics
- Salt and black ground pepper to taste
- 2 tablespoon of olive oil (or garlic-infused olive oil)
- 2 chicken sausages finely chopped
- 1 spring onion diced
- 1 cup of sweet peppers finely sliced
- 1 cup of fresh spinach, chopped
- ¼ teaspoon of ground paprika
- Tbsp of fresh parsley finely chopped

Directions:

1. IIn a mixing bowl, beat eggs with a pinch of the salt and pepper.
2. IAdd all remaining ingredients and stir well.
3. IFill 4 small cups to halfway with the egg mixture.
4. IBake soufflé with your air fryer at 400 F for about 6 to 8 minutes (it depends on your preference).
5. IServe hot and enjoy your breakfast and the rest of the day.

Nutritional Value (Amount per Serving):

Calories: 228; Fat: 17.54; Carb: 10.54; Protein: 7.61

Air Fryer Mushrooms-Parmesan Frittata

Prep Time: 15 Minutes
Cook Time: 30 Minutes
Serves: 4

Ingredients:

- 3 tablespoons of fresh butter
- 6 large eggs at room temperature
- ½ cup of shredded parmesan cheese
- ¼ cup of fresh cream
- 1 green onion finely chopped
- 1 teaspoon of fresh chopped thyme
- ¾ lb of button mushrooms, sliced
- Salt and ground black pepper

Directions:

1. IGrease with butter a 7-inch baking pan; set aside.
2. ICut mushrooms into slices.
3. IIn a bowl, whisk the eggs along with Parmesan, salt, thyme, and cream.
4. IHeat butter in a frying pan over medium heat.
5. ISauté the green onion with a pinch of salt and pepper until soft.
6. IAdd the mushrooms and cook for further two minutes; stir.
7. IRemove from the heat and allow it to cool for 5 minutes.
8. IPreheat your Air fryer to 350 F.
9. ICombine the egg mixture with the mushroom mixture and stir well.
10. IPour the mixture in a prepared baking pan and place inside the air fryer basket.
11. ICook for 13-16 minutes, or until eggs are set.
12. IAllow the frittata to cool for 10 to 15 minutes; slice and serve.

Nutritional Value (Amount per Serving):

Calories: 501; Fat: 22.73; Carb: 69.44; Protein: 16.65

Air Fryer Poppyseed Muffins

Prep Time: 10 Minutes
Cook Time: 50 Minutes
Serves: 12

Ingredients:

- Non-stick cooking spray
- 2 cups of almond flour
- 2 tablespoons of poppy seed
- 2 teaspoon of baking powder double acting
- 1 cup of granulated stevia sweetener or to taste
- eggs at room temperature
- ⅓ cup of heavy cream
- Tbsp of olive oil
- tsp of vanilla extract
- tsp of grated lemon zest
- Pinch of salt

Directions:

1. ISpray your silicone muffin tins with cooking spray; set aside.
2. IIn a mixing bowl, mix together all ingredients until combine well.
3. IFill prepared muffin cups about 3 of the way full.
4. ISet your air fryer for 320 F for about 13 to14 minutes.
5. ICook 4 to 5 muffins per batch.
6. IRemove from molds and allow to slightly cool.
7. IServe and enjoy your breakfast.

Nutritional Value (Amount per Serving):

Calories: 100; Fat: 3.96; Carb: 14.9; Protein: 1.14

Keto Air Fried Bacon Breakfast Omelet

Prep Time: 10 Minutes
Cook Time: 15 Minutes
Serves: 2

Ingredients:

- 1 teaspoon of lard
- 4 large eggs (room temperature)
- ¼ cup of Cheddar Cheese
- 4 slices bacon, cured and crumbled
- 4 stalks of fresh chives
- Salt and pepper to taste

Directions:

1. IGrease 2 ramekins with lard; set aside.
2. IIn a bowl beat eggs with Cheddar Cheese.
3. IAdd crumbled bacon and chives; stir well.
4. IDivide egg mixture between two ramekins.
5. IBake in your Air fryer at 330 F for 14-17 minutes.
6. IServe hot.

Nutritional Value (Amount per Serving):

Calories: 356; Fat: 31.92; Carb: 4.33; Protein: 12.91

Air Fryer Button Mushrooms With BBQ Sauce

Prep Time: 10 Minutes
Cook Time: 10 Minutes
Serves: 5

Ingredients:

- 1 ½ lb of fresh button mushrooms
- ½ cup of BBQ sauce
- 3 tablespoon of olive oil
- 2 teaspoon of garlic flakes
- 1 teaspoon of ground onion

Directions:

1. IIn a container, combine all ingredients and gently stir.
2. IAdd prepared mushrooms to a basket of Air fryer.
3. ICook mushrooms at 400 F for about 5 to 7 minutes.
4. IServe warm.

Nutritional Value (Amount per Serving):

Calories: 505; Fat: 9.55; Carb: 109.68; Protein: 14.04

Air Fryer Italian Sausages

Prep Time: 10 Minutes
Cook Time: 10 Minutes
Serves: 3

Ingredients:

- 1 lb of Italian smoked sausages
- 1 fresh lemon juice (2 lemons)
- Oregano (optional)

Directions:

1. IPreheat your Air fryer to 360 F.
2. IPrick holes into the sausages from all sides.
3. IPlace sausages into the Air fryer and cook for 13 to15 minutes.
4. IYour sausages are ready when the internal temperature reaches 165 F.
5. ISqueeze the lemon juice over the sausages.
6. ISprinkle with oregano and serve.

Nutritional Value (Amount per Serving):

Calories: 392; Fat: 27.5; Carb: 15.98; Protein: 28.07

Air-Fryer Wasabi Egg Salad Wraps

Prep Time: 10 Minutes
Cook Time: 35 Minutes
Serves: 4

Ingredients:

- 6 large eggs
- 1 ripe avocado
- 1 tablespoon lime juice
- 2 teaspoons wasabi sauce
- ¼ teaspoon salt
- ¼ teaspoon ground pepper
- ½ cup chopped cucumber
- 8 butterhead lettuce leaves
- Chopped fresh cilantro for garnish
- Lime wedges for serving

Directions:

1. IPreheat air fryer to 250°F for 5 minutes. Place eggs in the air-fryer basket; cook for 20 minutes. Immediately plunge the eggs into an ice bath. Let stand until cool, about 5 minutes. Drain, peel and coarsely chop the eggs.
2. IScoop avocado flesh into a medium bowl. Add lime juice and wasabi sauce to taste; mash until mostly smooth. Stir in salt and pepper. Fold in the chopped eggs and cucumber. Divide the mixture between lettuce leaves. If desired, sprinkle with cilantro and serve with lime wedges.

Nutritional Value (Amount per Serving):

Calories: 256; Fat: 18.59; Carb: 7.88; Protein: 15.75

Air Fryer Sweet Potato Hash

Prep Time: 10 Minutes
Cook Time: 15 Minutes
Serves: 6

Ingredients:

- 2 large sweet potato, cut into small cubes
- 2 slices bacon, cut into small pieces
- 2 tablespoons olive oil
- 1 tablespoon smoked paprika
- 1 teaspoon sea salt
- 1 teaspoon ground black pepper
- 1 teaspoon dried dill weed

Directions:

1. IPreheat an air fryer to 400 degrees F.
2. IToss sweet potato, bacon, olive oil, paprika, salt, pepper, and dill in a large bowl. Place mixture into the preheated air fryer. Cook for 12 to 16 minutes. Check and stir after 10 minutes, and then every 3 minutes until crispy and browned.

Nutritional Value (Amount per Serving):

Calories: 134; Fat: 8.16; Carb: 13.15; Protein: 2.54

Fryer Bacon

Prep Time: 5 Minutes

Cook Time: 15 Minutes

Serves: 6

Ingredients:

- ½ (16 ounce) package bacon

Directions:

1. IPreheat an air fryer to 390 degrees F according to manufacturer's instructions.
2. ILay bacon in the air fryer basket in a single layer; some overlap is okay.

Nutritional Value (Amount per Serving):

Calories: 117; Fat: 11.16; Carb: 2.39; Protein: 4.04

Air Fryer Breakfast Frittata

Prep Time: 15 Minutes
Cook Time: 20 Minutes
Serves: 2

Ingredients:

- cooking spray
- ¼ pound breakfast sausage, fully cooked and crumbled
- 4 large eggs, lightly beaten
- ½ cup shredded Cheddar-Monterey Jack cheese blend
- 2 tablespoons red bell pepper, diced
- 1 green onion, chopped
- 1 pinch cayenne pepper (Optional)

Directions:

1. IPreheat an air fryer to 360 degrees F. Spray a nonstick 6x2-inch cake pan with cooking spray.
2. ICombine sausage, eggs, cheese, bell pepper, green onion, and cayenne pepper in a large bowl; mix well to combine.
3. IPour egg mixture into the prepared cake pan.
4. ICook in the preheated air fryer until frittata is set, 18 to 20 minutes.

Nutritional Value (Amount per Serving):

Calories: 382; Fat: 25.95; Carb: 19.9; Protein: 16.82

Tex-Mex Air Fryer Hash Browns

Prep Time: 15 Minutes
Cook Time: 30 Minutes
Serves: 4

Ingredients:

- 1 ½ pounds potatoes, peeled and cut into 1-inch cubes
- 1 tablespoon olive oil
- 1 red bell pepper, seeded and cut into 1-inch pieces
- 1 small onion, cut into 1-inch pieces
- 1 jalapeno, seeded and cut into 1-inch rings
- ½ teaspoon olive oil
- ½ teaspoon taco seasoning mix
- ½ teaspoon ground cumin
- 1 pinch salt and ground black pepper to taste

Directions:

1. ISoak potatoes in cool water for 20 minutes.
2. IPreheat the air fryer to 320 degrees F. Drain the potatoes, dry them with a clean towel, and transfer to a large bowl. Drizzle 1 tablespoon olive oil over the potatoes and toss to coat. Add them to the preheated air fryer basket. Set the timer for 18 minutes.
3. IPut bell pepper, onion, and jalapeno in the bowl previously used for the potatoes. Sprinkle in 1/2 teaspoon olive oil, taco seasoning, ground cumin, salt, and pepper. Toss to coat.
4. ITransfer potatoes from the air fryer to the bowl with the vegetable mixture. Return the empty basket to the air fryer and raise the temperature to 356 degrees F.
5. IQuickly toss the contents of the bowl to mix the potatoes evenly with the vegetables and seasoning. Transfer mixture into the basket. Cook for 6 minutes, shake the basket, and continue cooking until potatoes are browned and crispy, about 5 more minutes. Serve immediately.

Nutritional Value (Amount per Serving):

Calories: 196; Fat: 4.89; Carb: 33.75; Protein: 5.61

Air Fryer Sausage Patties

Prep Time: 5 Minutes
Cook Time: 10 Minutes
Serves: 4

Ingredients:

- 1 (12 ounce) package sausage patties (such as Johnsonville®)
- 1 serving nonstick cooking spray

Directions:

1. IGrab your ingredients, and preheat an air fryer to 400 degrees F. Lightly grease the inside of the air fryer basket with nonstick spray.
2. IArrange sausage patties in a single layer in the air fryer basket.
3. ICook in the preheated air fryer for 5 minutes; flip the patties and cook about 3 more minutes. An instant-read thermometer inserted into the center of a patty should read at least 160 degrees F.
4. IServe hot and enjoy!

Nutritional Value (Amount per Serving):

Calories: 40; Fat: 0.15; Carb: 10.27; Protein: 0.41

Air Fryer Breakfast Toad-in-the-Hole Tarts

Prep Time: 5 Minutes
Cook Time: 25 Minutes
Serves: 4

Ingredients:

- 1 sheet frozen puff pastry, thawed
- 4 tablespoons shredded Cheddar cheese
- 4 tablespoons diced cooked ham
- 4 eggs
- 1 tablespoon chopped fresh chives

Directions:

1. IPreheat the air fryer to 400 degrees F.
2. IUnfold pastry sheet on a flat surface and cut into 4 squares.
3. IPlace 2 pastry squares in the air fryer basket and cook 6 to 8 minutes.
4. IRemove basket from air fryer. Use a metal tablespoon to press each square gently to form an indentation. Place 1 tablespoon of Cheddar cheese and 1 tablespoon ham in each hole, and pour 1 egg on top of each.
5. IReturn basket to air fryer. Cook to desired doneness, about 6 more minutes. Remove tarts from basket and let cool 5 minutes. Repeat with remaining pastry squares, cheese, ham, and eggs.
6. IGarnish tarts with chives.

Nutritional Value (Amount per Serving):

Calories: 447; Fat: 22.83; Carb: 9.65; Protein: 50.06

Chapter 2:
Desserts and Snacks

Air Fryer Almond Breaded Asparagus

Prep Time: 10 Minutes
Cook Time: 10 Minutes
Serves: 4

Ingredients:

- 1 lb of raw asparagus cleaned
- ½ cup of ground almonds
- 1 large egg beaten
- ½ cup of parmesan cheese grated
- 2 tablespoon olive of olive oil
- Salt and ground pepper to taste

Directions:

1. IRinse, and trim the ends of the asparagus from the bottom.
2. IIn a bowl add ground almonds.
3. IIn a separate bowl, beat the egg with a pinch of salt.
4. IIn a third bowl, combine together parmesan cheese with the salt and pepper.
5. IDip every part of asparagus in ground almond, then in the egg mixture and at last in parmesan cheese.
6. IPlace the asparagus on a baking tray.
7. IPlace the asparagus into your Air fryer basket and then close.
8. ITurn the fryer to 400 F, and cook for 7 to 8 minutes.
9. IRemove asparagus on a serving plate and serve.

Nutritional Value (Amount per Serving):

Calories: 154; Fat: 11.59; Carb: 7.39; Protein: 6.98

Air-Fryer Crispy Chickpeas

Prep Time: 20 Minutes
Cook Time: 20 Minutes
Serves: 4

Ingredients:

- 1 (15 ounce) can unsalted chickpeas, rinsed and drained
- 1 ½ tablespoons toasted sesame oil
- ¼ teaspoon smoked paprika
- ¼ teaspoon crushed red pepper
- ⅛ teaspoon salt
- Cooking spray
- 2 lime wedges

Directions:

1. ISpread chickpeas on several layers of paper towels. Top with more paper towels and pat until very dry, rolling the chickpeas under the paper towels to dry all sides.
2. ICombine the chickpeas and oil in a medium bowl. Sprinkle with paprika, crushed red pepper and salt. Pour into an air fryer basket and coat with cooking spray. Cook at 400 degrees F until very well browned, 12 to 14 minutes, shaking the basket occasionally. Squeeze lime wedges over the chickpeas and serve.

Nutritional Value (Amount per Serving):

Calories: 177; Fat: 7.31; Carb: 23.02; Protein: 6.93

Cheesy Zucchini Tots

Prep Time: 20 Minutes
Cook Time: 20 Minutes
Serves: 4

Ingredients:

- 1 medium-large zucchini (about 12 ounces)
- 1 ounce provolone cheese (about 1/3 cup shredded)
- 1 ounce fontina cheese (about 1/3 cup shredded)
- 1 ounce Parmesan cheese (about 1/4 cup grated)
- ½ cup panko breadcrumbs (regular or gluten-free)
- 2 tablespoons all-purpose flour or gluten-free flour blend
- ½ teaspoon ground pepper
- ½ teaspoon dried oregano
- 1 large egg, beaten
- Cooking spray

Directions:

1. IPreheat oven or air fryer to 400°F. If baking, line a large rimmed baking sheet with parchment paper or a silicone liner.
2. IShred zucchini on the coarse side of a box grater. Place the shredded zucchini in a clean cotton towel (not terry cloth) and squeeze tightly to release excess liquid. Place in a large bowl. Shred provolone and fontina into the bowl, then grate Parmesan into the bowl. Add panko, flour, pepper and oregano; stir to combine. Add egg and stir to coat well.
3. IUsing your hands, lightly squeeze generous 1 1/2-tablespoon portions of the zucchini mixture to create 1-by-1 1/2-inch tots. You should have 28 tots.
4. IIf baking, place on the prepared baking sheet and lightly coat with cooking spray. Bake until lightly browned and crispy on top, about 20 minutes. If air-frying, coat the air-fryer basket and the tops of the tots with cooking spray. Air-fry until lightly browned and crispy on top, about 6 minutes.
5. ILet the tots rest for 4 minutes before serving with your favorite sauce.

Nutritional Value (Amount per Serving):

Calories: 128; Fat: 7.36; Carb: 8.21; Protein: 7.25

Air Fryer Coconut-Pecan Nuts Snack

Prep Time: 10 Minutes
Cook Time: 10 Minutes
Serves: 6

Ingredients:

- 3 tablespoons of coconut oil melted
- 4 drops of liquid stevia sweetener
- 1 teaspoon of pure vanilla extract (no alcohol)
- ¼ teaspoon of ground allspice
- 1 ½ teaspoon of ground cinnamon
- 16 oz of pecan halves

Directions:

1. IIn a bowl, combine together the first 5 ingredients until you have a thick mixture.
Stir in your pecans.
2. ITransfer the pecans to your air fryer basket, and cook at 320 F for 6-8 minutes.
3. IStir every 2 minutes to prevent sticking.
4. ILet them cool to room temperature about 10 minutes.
5. IKeep them in an airtight container at room temperature for 5 days.

Nutritional Value (Amount per Serving):

Calories: 638; Fat: 61.23; Carb: 25.53; Protein: 6.96

Air Fryer Keto Pumpkin Pie (Crustless)

Prep Time: 10 Minutes
Cook Time: 35 Minutes
Serves: 6

Ingredients:

- Cooking spray, as needed
- 3 large eggs at room temperature
- 1 can (11 oz) of pumpkin pure unsalted, unsweetened
- 2 teaspoon organic pumpkin pie spice
- 1 cup heavy cream
- ¼ teaspoon grated nutmeg
- ½ cup of stevia powdered sugar
- ¼ cup of Parmesan cheese
- Salt and ground white pepper to taste

Directions:

1. IPreheat Air Fryer to 350 F.
2. IGrease your air fryer pan with cooking spray, and set aside.
3. IPlace all ingredients together in a large mixing bowl.
4. IStir with an electric mixer until all ingredients combined well.
5. IPour the mixture in the prepared air fryer pan.
6. ICook in the Air Fryer for 35 minutes.
7. IRemove from oven and let it cool at room temperature.
8. IRefrigerate for several hours, slice and serve.

Nutritional Value (Amount per Serving):

Calories: 217; Fat: 13.78; Carb: 18.79; Protein: 5.85

Keto Cheesy Chicken And Vegetable Pie (Air Fryer)

Prep Time: 10 Minutes
Cook Time: 15 Minutes
Serves: 6

Ingredients:

- 3 tablespoons of olive oil
- 1 green onion finely chopped
- 2 cloves garlic minced
- 1 cup of cooked broccoli
- 1 cup of chicken breast cut in small cubes
- 4 egg whites, beaten
- ¾ cup of grated Parmesan or Cheddar cheese
- 1 cup of goat cheese crumbled
- 1 teaspoon of baking soda
- 1 teaspoon of baking powder double acting
- 1 teaspoon of fresh basil finely chopped salt to taste

Directions:

1. IPreheat your Air Fryer to 320 F.
2. ISpray your Air Fryer baking pan and set aside.
3. IAdd all ingredients into mixing bowl.
4. IBeat until all ingredients are combined well or until a smooth mixture is achieved.

   Pour the mixture in a prepared baking pan and sprinkle with some extra parmesan cheese.

5. ICook for 12 to 13 minutes.
6. IRemove pie from the air fryer, and let it cool slightly
7. IReady! Serve.

Nutritional Value (Amount per Serving):

Calories: 201; Fat: 15.75; Carb: 3.42; Protein: 11.91

Greek Keto Air Fryer Calamari Rings

Prep Time: 10 Minutes
Cook Time: 10 Minutes
Serves: 4

Ingredients:

- 1 lb of calamari rings
- 1 cup of almond flour
- 2 eggs beaten
- 1 tablespoon of fresh lemon juice
- 1 lemon rind
- 1 tablespoon of spicy paprika
- 1 tablespoon of fresh basil finely chopped
- 1 teaspoon of fresh parsley finely chopped
- Salt and ground black pepper
- Lemon slices for serving

Directions:

1. IPreheat your air fryer to 360 F.
2. IIn a bowl, place the almond flour.
3. IIn a separate bowl, beat the eggs with the pinch of salt.
4. IGenerously sprinkle your calamari rings with the salt, pepper, and lemon.
5. IPlace your calamari rings first into the almond meal, then into the egg mixture.
6. IPlace in your air fryer and cook for 8 minutes.
7. IServe with lemon slices and enjoy!

Nutritional Value (Amount per Serving):

Calories: 395; Fat: 21.5; Carb: 42.83; Protein: 9.84

Air Fryer Cheesy Coconut Cookies

Prep Time: 10 Minutes
Cook Time: 25 Minutes
Serves: 12

Ingredients:

- ¼ cup of softened cream cheese
- ½ cup of fresh butter softened, unsalted
- ½ cup of stevia granulated sweetener
- 1 teaspoon of pure vanilla extract (no alcohol)
- 1 egg at room temperature
- ½ teaspoon of baking soda
- ½ cup of coconut flour
- Pinch of salt
- Shredded Cheddar cheese (optional)

Directions:

1. IPreheat Air fryer to 350 F.
2. ILine fryer basket with foil.
3. IIn a bowl, stir together the butter, stevia sweetener and softened cream cheese.
4. IStir the vanilla extract and egg until combined well.
5. IAdd the coconut flour, salt, and baking soda; continue to stir until combined well.
6. IPlace the batter onto a plate lined with baking paper.
7. IForm into a log shape, using the paper to roll out and wrap the paper around the dough.
8. IUse a sharp knife to cut any shape of cookie you like.
9. IPlace cookies on lined Air basket and sprinkle with cheddar cheese (if used).
10. IAir fry for 10 minutes or until golden.
11. IKeep refrigerated into the closed container up to 4 to 5 days.

Nutritional Value (Amount per Serving):

Calories: 96; Fat: 9.93; Carb: 1.86; Protein: 1.25

Air Fryer Keto Almond Cookies

Prep Time: 10 Minutes
Cook Time: 15 Minutes
Serves: 4

Ingredients:

- 2 cups of ground almonds unsalted
- ½ cup of stevia granulated sweetener (or to taste)
- 2 tablespoon of grated lemon rind
- 1 pinch of salt
- 1 large egg at room temperature
- Cooking spray
- 1 teaspoon of ground cinnamon
- 24 whole blanched almonds

Directions:

1. IPreheat Air fryer to 350 F.
2. ILine fryer basket with foil.
3. IAdd all ingredients into the food processor; process until well combined into smooth dough.
4. IShape dough into 24 small balls, and gently press one whole almond into the center of each dough ball.
5. IPlace almond balls on a prepared fryer basket.
6. IAir- fry until lightly golden brown, 8-10 minutes.
7. ICool completely on wire racks and serve.

Nutritional Value (Amount per Serving):

Calories: 535; Fat: 48.06; Carb: 20.18; Protein: 18.92

Keto Choco Cake (Air Fryer)

Prep Time: 10 Minutes
Cook Time: 15 Minutes
Serves: 8

Ingredients:

- 2 cups of almond flour
- ¼ cup of cocoa powder unsweetened
- ⅛ teaspoon baking soda
- ⅛ teaspoon salt
- ½ cup of coconut oil, melted
- 2 tablespoons of almond milk (unsweetened)
- 2 teaspoons of pure vanilla extract
- 1 tablespoon of water
- ⅓ cup of granulated stevia sweetener (or to taste)

Directions:

1. ICombine the cocoa powder, almond flour, salt and baking soda in a bowl.
2. IIn a separate bowl, whisk together melted coconut oil, almond milk, water, vanilla extract, and granulated stevia.
3. ICombine the almond flour mixture with the almond milk mixture and stir well.
4. IPlace batter in Air fry basket.
5. IProgram Cake setting 330 F for 9 to 10 minutes.
6. IAllow it to cool completely, slice and serve.
7. IEnjoy!

Nutritional Value (Amount per Serving):

Calories: 130; Fat: 14.25; Carb: 3.12; Protein: 0.67

Simple Keto Vanilla Cookies (Air Fryer)

Prep Time: 10 Minutes
Cook Time: 15 Minutes
Serves: 4

Ingredients:

- 3 cups of almond flour or finely chopped almonds
- ⅔ cup of fresh unsalted butter
- 2 cups of stevia granulated powder (or to taste)
- 2 eggs, at room temperature
- 1 ¼ teaspoon of pure vanilla extract (no alcohol)
- 1 teaspoon of cinnamon
- 2 teaspoons baking powder
- 1 teaspoon of baking powder, double-acting
- 2 tablespoons of water
- Sea salt

Directions:

1. IPreheat your Air fryer to 350 F.
2. ILine Air fryer basket with foil.
3. IIn a bowl, beat the butter with granulated stevia sweetener.
4. IAdd eggs, water and vanilla extract; continue to beat.
5. IAdd all remaining ingredients and stir until a smooth dough is achieved.
6. IForm into balls using 1 tablespoon of dough (about 24 cookies); flatten slightly.
7. IPlace cookies into prepared Air basket.
8. IAir fry for about 8 - 10 minutes or until cookies are lightly browned.
9. IRemove to wire racks.
10. IServe warm or cold; store in a container and keep refrigerated up to 5 days.

Nutritional Value (Amount per Serving):

Calories: 694; Fat: 46.41; Carb: 55.73; Protein: 17.13

Air-Fryer Potato Cakes

Prep Time: 15 Minutes
Cook Time: 45 Minutes
Serves: 4

Ingredients:

- 1 ½ pounds Yukon Gold potatoes, peeled and cubed
- 1 large egg
- 1 tablespoon unsalted butter, melted
- ½ teaspoon salt
- Cooking spray

Directions:

1. IBring a large pot of water to a boil. Add potatoes and cook until fork-tender, 20 to 25 minutes. Drain and transfer to a large bowl; set aside to cool for 15 minutes.
2. IMash the potatoes with a potato masher. Add egg, butter and salt; mix well. Form 1/4-cup portions of the mixture into 3-inch-diameter cakes. Place the cakes on a baking sheet or tray and refrigerate for 15 minutes.
3. ITransfer the potato cakes to the basket of an air fryer; coat with cooking spray. Cook at 400°F, flipping once, until golden brown and edges are crisp, 12 to 16 minutes. Top as desired.

Nutritional Value (Amount per Serving):

Calories: 162; Fat: 3.21; Carb: 29.87; Protein: 4.23

Air Fryer Apple Fritters

Prep Time: 15 Minutes
Cook Time: 10 Minutes
Serves: 4

Ingredients:

- cooking spray
- 1 cup all-purpose flour
- ¼ cup white sugar
- ¼ cup milk
- 1 egg
- 1 ½ teaspoons baking powder
- 1 pinch salt
- 2 tablespoons white sugar
- ½ teaspoon ground cinnamon
- 1 apple - peeled, cored, and chopped
- ½ cup confectioners› sugar
- 1 tablespoon milk
- ½ teaspoon caramel extract (such as Watkins™)
- ¼ teaspoon ground cinnamon

Directions:

1. IPreheat an air fryer to 350 degrees F. Place a parchment paper round into the bottom of the air fryer. Spray with nonstick cooking spray.
2. IMix flour, 1/4 cup sugar, milk, egg, baking powder, and salt together in a small bowl. Stir until combined.
3. IMix 2 tablespoons sugar with cinnamon in another bowl and sprinkle over apples until coated. Mix apples into the flour mixture until combined.
4. IDrop fritters using a cookie scoop onto the bottom of the air fryer basket.
5. IAir-fry in the preheated fryer for 5 minutes. Flip fritters and cook until golden, about 5 minutes more.
6. IMeanwhile, mix confectioners' sugar, milk, caramel extract, and cinnamon together in a bowl. Transfer fritters to a cooling rack and drizzle with glaze.

Nutritional Value (Amount per Serving):

Calories: 277; Fat: 5.84; Carb: 50.69; Protein: 6.57

Air Fryer Donut Sticks

Prep Time: 20 Minutes
Cook Time: 15 Minutes
Serves: 8

Ingredients:

- 1 (8 ounce) package refrigerated crescent roll dough
- ¼ cup unsalted butter, melted
- ½ cup white sugar
- 2 teaspoons ground cinnamon
- ½ cup any flavor fruit jam

Directions:

1. IUnroll crescent roll dough and press into an 8x12-inch rectangle. Cut in half lengthwise with a pizza cutter, then cut each piece crosswise into 1/2-inch-wide strips.
2. IWorking in batches, dip strips in melted butter and place in a single layer in the air fryer basket without overcrowding.
3. ICook in the air fryer at 380 degrees F until well browned, 4 to 5 minutes per batch.
4. IWhile the doughnut sticks are cooking, stir sugar and cinnamon together in a pie plate or shallow bowl.
5. IRemove doughnut sticks from the air fryer and roll in cinnamon-sugar mixture. Serve with jam.

Nutritional Value (Amount per Serving):

Calories: 569; Fat: 29.59; Carb: 74.95; Protein: 9.45

Chapter 3: Poultry

Air Fried BBQ Turkey Patties

Prep Time: 10 Minutes
Cook Time: 20 Minutes
Serves: 4

Ingredients:

- 1 ½ lbs of ground turkey
- ½ cup of green onion finely chopped
- ½ cup of BBQ sauce (unsweetened; check the label)
- ½ cup of almond flour or ground almonds
- ½ teaspoon salt and ground black pepper to taste

Directions:

1. IIn a large bowl or container, combine all ingredients.
2. IStir thoroughly or knead with your hands: shape the mixture into 6 patties.
3. ISpray the air fryer basket with cooking spray, and place burgers into a single layer.
4. IClose the lid, and choose 360 F; cook for 13 to 15 minutes (your burgers are done when internal temperature reaches 165 F)
5. IRemove from basket and serve hot.

Nutritional Value (Amount per Serving):

Calories: 272; Fat: 13.2; Carb: 4.48; Protein: 34.29

Air-Fryer Rotisserie Chicken

Prep Time: 10 Minutes
Cook Time: 60 Minutes
Serves: 6

Ingredients:

- 4 sprigs fresh thyme
- 1 lemon, halved
- 1 (3 1/2 to 4 pound) whole chicken, giblets removed
- ¾ teaspoon salt, divided
- ½ teaspoon ground pepper, divided

Directions:

1. IPlace thyme sprigs and lemon halves in chicken cavity. Truss the chicken legs closed with kitchen twine. Sprinkle the breasts and legs evenly with 3/8 teaspoon salt and 1/4 teaspoon pepper. Place the chicken, breast-side up, in the air-fryer basket.
2. ISet the air fryer to 350°F (no need to preheat); cook for 30 minutes. Carefully turn the chicken over; cook for 15 minutes. Carefully turn the chicken over again; cook until a thermometer inserted in the thickest portion of a thigh registers 165 degrees F, 10 to 15 minutes. Transfer the chicken to a cutting board; let rest for 10 minutes.
3. ICarve the chicken; discard the thyme and reserve the lemon halves. Sprinkle the chicken evenly with the remaining 3/8 teaspoon salt and 1/4 teaspoon pepper; squeeze the juice from the reserved lemon halves over the chicken.

Nutritional Value (Amount per Serving):

Calories: 206; Fat: 4.44; Carb: 17.21; Protein: 28.6

Air-Fryer Drumsticks

Prep Time: 10 Minutes
Cook Time: 25 Minutes
Serves: 4

Ingredients:

- 4 chicken drumsticks (about 1 1/2 lbs. total)
- 1 tablespoon extra-virgin olive oil
- 1 tablespoon brown sugar
- 1 tablespoon smoked paprika
- 1 teaspoon grated lime zest
- 1 teaspoon garlic powder
- ½ teaspoon onion powder
- ½ teaspoon salt
- ½ teaspoon ground pepper

Directions:

1. IPat chicken dry with paper towels. Transfer to a medium bowl. Drizzle the chicken evenly with oil and toss to coat. Add brown sugar and toss to coat. Combine paprika, lime zest, garlic powder, onion powder, salt and pepper in a small bowl. Sprinkle evenly over the chicken; toss to coat. Let stand at room temperature for 10 minutes.
2. IMeanwhile, preheat air fryer to 375°F for about 5 minutes. Lightly coat the air-fryer basket with cooking spray.
3. IArrange the chicken, skin-side down, in a single layer in the basket; cook for 10 minutes. Flip and cook until the skin is crispy and a thermometer inserted into the thickest portion registers 165°F, 10 to 15 minutes.

Nutritional Value (Amount per Serving):

Calories: 242; Fat: 13.7; Carb: 4.49; Protein: 24.04

Air Fryer Lemon And Garlic Chicken Breast

Prep Time: 10 Minutes
Cook Time: 20 Minutes
Serves: 4

Ingredients:

- 1 ½ lbs of chicken breasts, bone-in
- Sea salt and white ground pepper to taste
- 2 tablespoon of coconut oil melted
- 2 tablespoon of olive oil
- 2 teaspoons of minced garlic
- ½ cup of lemon juice
- 2 teaspoons of lemon rind
- 1 teaspoon of fresh parsley finely chopped

Directions:

1. IAdd chicken breast into container and season with the salt and ground white pepper.
2. IIn a separate bowl, combine all remaining ingredients and pour over chicken; cover and toss to combine well.
3. IRefrigerate for 2 hours (or more).
4. IPreheat your Air fryer to 360 F.
5. IPlace chicken breast into the air fryer basket.
6. ICook for 20 minutes (10 minutes per side).
7. IRemove chicken breasts onto a serving plate and allow them to rest for 10 minutes.

Nutritional Value (Amount per Serving):

Calories: 425; Fat: 29.4; Carb: 3.83; Protein: 35.91

Air Fried Cheesy Chicken Wings

Prep Time: 10 Minutes
Cook Time: 15 Minutes
Serves: 4

Ingredients:

- 20 chicken wings
- 2 tablespoons of garlic-infused olive oil
- 1 cup of grated parmesan cheese
- 1 teaspoon chives, chopped
- Salt and ground pepper to taste
- Lemon wedges for serving

Directions:

1. IPlace chicken wings in a mixing bowl.
2. IIn a separate bowl, combine together all remaining ingredients.
3. ISprinkle the mixture over chicken wings and toss to combine well.
4. IPlace chicken wings on the frying basket in a single layer, spacing evenly.
5. IAir fry at 400 F for a total of 16 minutes or for 8 minutes per side.
6. IServe hot with lemon wedges.

Nutritional Value (Amount per Serving):

Calories: 355; Fat: 18.9; Carb: 5.38; Protein: 39.24

Air Fryer Chicken Breast With Mustard And Herbs

Prep Time: 10 Minutes
Cook Time: 25 Minutes
Serves: 4

Ingredients:

- 2 tablespoons of olive oil
- 3 cloves of minced garlic
- 3 tablespoons of stone-ground mustard (gluten-free)
- ½ teaspoon of fresh parsley, finely chopped
- ¼ teaspoon of fresh tarragon, finely chopped
- ¼ tablespoon of dried oregano
- Sea salt and ground black pepper to taste
- 4 chicken breasts, boneless and skinless

Directions:

1. IPreheat Air Fryer to 390 F(for 5 minutes).
2. ICombine all ingredients and rub evenly over chicken breasts.
3. IPlace the chicken pieces in the basket in a single layer.
4. ICook in Air Fryer for 25 minutes.
5. ILet cool before slicing; serve.

Nutritional Value (Amount per Serving):

Calories: 591; Fat: 35.33; Carb: 3.17; Protein: 62.08

Low Carb Keto Paleo Baked Chicken Nuggets

Prep Time: 10 Minutes
Cook Time: 15 Minutes
Serves: 4

Ingredients:

- 1 Pound Free-range boneless, skinless chicken breast
- Pinch sea salt
- 1 tsp Sesame oil
- 1/4 Cup Coconut flour
- 1/2 tsp Ground ginger
- 4 Egg whites
- 6 Tbsp Toasted sesame seeds
- Cooking spray of choice
- 2 Tbsp Natural creamy almond butter
- 4 tsp Coconut aminos (or GF soy sauce)
- 1 Tbsp Water
- 2 tsp Rice vinegar
- 1 tsp Sriracha, or to taste
- 1/2 tsp Ground ginger
- 1/2 tsp Monkfruit (omit for whole30)

Directions:

1. IPreheat you air fryer to 400 degrees for 10 minutes.
2. IWhile the air fryer heats, cut the chicken into nuggets (about 1 inch pieces,) dry them off and place them in a bowl. Toss with salt and sesame oil until coated.
3. IPlace the coconut flour and ground ginger in a large Ziploc bag and shake to combine. Add the chicken and shake until coated.
4. IPlace the egg whites in a large bowl and add in the chicken nuggets, tossing until they are all well coated in the egg.
5. IPlace the sesame seeds in a large, Ziploc bag. Shake any excess egg off the chicken and add the nuggets into the bag, shake until well coated.

6. IGENEROUSLY spray the mesh air fryer basket with cooking spray. Place the nuggets into the basket,making sure to not crowd them or they won't get crispy. Spray with a touch of cooking spray.

7. ICook for 6 minutes. Flip each nugget and spray for cooking spray. Then, cook an additional 5-6 minutes until no longer pink inside, with a crispy outside.

8. IWhile the nuggets cook, whisk all the sauce ingredients together in a medium bowl until smooth.

9. IServe the nuggets with the dip and DEVOUR!

Nutritional Value (Amount per Serving):

Calories: 273; Fat: 15.41; Carb: 4.29; Protein: 31.12

Air Fryer French Onion Chicken Breast

Prep Time: 10 Minutes
Cook Time: 10 Minutes
Serves: 2

Ingredients:

- 1 large onion sliced
- 2 tablespoons olive oil
- 1 teaspoon granulated sugar
- 1 teaspoon kosher salt
- 1/2 teaspoon kosher salt
- 2 boneless, skinless chicken breast
- 2 teaspoons olive oil
- 1/2 teaspoon kosher salt
- 1/2 teaspoon kosher salt
- 2-3 ounces Fontina cheese sliced

Directions:

1. IStart by slicing the onions into thin slices
2. IToss the sliced onions with olive oil, sugar and salt, and pepper in a small bowl. Then spread the coated onions in either the air fryer basket or in the air fryer tray, set the temperature to 350 degrees F for 5-7 minutes. (air fryer setting)
3. ICoat your chicken breast with olive oil, season with salt and pepper, and air fry your chicken breast for about 7-9 minutes at 350 degrees F. (air fryer setting)
4. ITop the chicken with the caramelized onions.
5. ITop the caramelized onions with the sliced fontina cheese, place in the air fryer for about 1-2 minutes, at 350 degrees F, air fryer setting, until the cheese is just melted.
6. IPlate, serve, and enjoy!

Nutritional Value (Amount per Serving):

Calories: 615; Fat: 35.3; Carb: 8.8; Protein: 63

Air Fryer Boneless Turkey Breast Roast

Prep Time: 10 Minutes
Cook Time: 30 Minutes
Serves: 6

Ingredients:

- 2-4 pounds boneless turkey breast casing remove
- 3 tablespoons rosemary
- 3 tablespoons Herbes de Provence
- 4 tablespoons olive oil
- 1 teaspoon salt
- 1/2 teaspoon black pepper

Directions:

1. IPlace your turkey roast on the air fryer tray.
2. IIn a small mixing bowl, mix the olive oil, rosemary, Herbes de Provence, salt, and black pepper.
3. IRub the mixture over the turkey roast.
4. ISet into the air fryer for 15 minutes at 350 degrees F.
5. IThen remove the roast and baste it with some more olive oil, air fry for another 10-15 minutes.
6. IThe roast is done when the internal temperature reaches 170 degrees F. The actual time will depend on the air fryer you own and how large your roast it. Larger roasts will take longer to air fry.
7. IPlate, serve, and enjoy!

Nutritional Value (Amount per Serving):

Calories: 415; Fat: 13.78; Carb: 0.35; Protein: 68.39

Mexican-Style Air Fryer Stuffed Chicken Breasts

Prep Time: 20 Minutes
Cook Time: 10 Minutes
Serves: 2

Ingredients:

- 4 extra-long toothpicks
- 4 teaspoons chili powder, divided
- 4 teaspoons ground cumin, divided
- 1 skinless, boneless chicken breast
- 2 teaspoons chipotle flakes
- 2 teaspoons Mexican oregano
- salt and ground black pepper to taste
- ½ red bell pepper, sliced into thin strips
- ½ onion, sliced into thin strips
- 1 fresh jalapeno pepper, sliced into thin strips
- 2 teaspoons corn oil
- ½ lime, juiced

Directions:

1. IPlace toothpicks in a small bowl and cover with water; let them soak to keep them from burning while cooking.
2. IMix 2 teaspoons chili powder and 2 teaspoons cumin in a shallow dish.
3. IPreheat an air fryer to 400 degrees F.
4. IPlace chicken breast on a flat work surface. Slice horizontally through the middle. Pound each half using a kitchen mallet or rolling pin until about 1/4-inch thick.
5. ISprinkle each breast half equally with remaining chili powder, remaining cumin, chipotle flakes, oregano, salt, and pepper. Place 1/2 the bell pepper, onion, and jalapeno in the center of 1 breast half. Roll the chicken from the tapered end upward and use 2 toothpicks to secure. Repeat with other breast, spices, and vegetables and secure with remaining toothpicks. Roll each roll-up in the chili-cumin mixture in the shallow dish while drizzling with

olive oil until evenly covered.

6. IPlace roll-ups in the air-fryer basket with the toothpick side facing up. Set timer for 6 minutes.

7. ITurn roll-ups over. Continue cooking in the air fryer until juices run clear and an instant-read thermometer inserted into the center reads at least 165 degrees F, about 5 more minutes.

8. IDrizzle lime juice evenly on roll-ups before serving.

Nutritional Value (Amount per Serving):

Calories: 266; Fat: 9.65; Carb: 16.39; Protein: 30.05

Air Fryer Blackened Chicken Breasts

Prep Time: 10 Minutes
Cook Time: 20 Minutes
Serves: 2

Ingredients:

- 2 teaspoons paprika
- 1 teaspoon ground thyme
- 1 teaspoon cumin
- ½ teaspoon cayenne pepper
- ½ teaspoon onion powder
- ½ teaspoon black pepper
- ¼ teaspoon salt
- 2 teaspoons vegetable oil
- 2 (6 ounce) skinless, boneless chicken breast halves

Directions:

1. IMix paprika, thyme, cumin, cayenne, onion powder, black pepper, and salt together in a bowl; transfer to a large plate.
2. IPreheat the air fryer to 360 degrees F.
3. IRub oil over each chicken breast until fully coated, then press into spice mixture until all sides are coated. Let sit for 5 minutes while the air fryer preheats. Place into the air fryer basket.
4. IAir-fry chicken until no longer pink in the center and the juices run clear, about 20 minutes, flipping halfway through. An instant-read thermometer inserted into the center should read at least 165 degrees F.
5. ITransfer chicken to a plate and let rest for 5 minutes before serving.

Nutritional Value (Amount per Serving):

Calories: 339; Fat: 11.33; Carb: 3.01; Protein: 53.83

Air Fryer Chicken Fajitas

Prep Time: 10 Minutes

Cook Time: 30 Minutes

Serves: 8

Ingredients:

- 1 medium red bell pepper, cut into thin strips
- 1 medium green bell pepper, cut into thin strips
- 1 large onion, sliced into petals
- 3 teaspoons olive oil, divided
- salt and pepper to taste
- 1 pound chicken tenders, cut into strips
- 2 teaspoons fajita seasoning
- 8 (6 inch) flour tortillas, warmed

Directions:

1. IPlace bell pepper strips and onion petals in a large bowl. Drizzle 2 teaspoons of olive oil over top and season with salt and pepper. Stir until evenly combined.
2. IPlace chicken strips in a separate bowl and sprinkle with fajita seasoning. Drizzle with remaining 1 teaspoon olive oil and mix until evenly combined with your hands.
3. IPreheat an air fryer to 350 degrees F. Add chicken to the basket and cook for 12 minutes, shaking halfway through cook time. Transfer to a plate to let rest while you cook the vegetables.
4. IAdd vegetable mixture to the basket of the air fryer and cook for 14 minutes, shaking halfway through cook time.
5. IDivide chicken and vegetable mixture among tortillas.

Nutritional Value (Amount per Serving):

Calories: 234; Fat: 6.06; Carb: 28.18; Protein: 15.86

Chapter 4: Beef and Pork

Air Fryer Mediterranean Meatballs

Prep Time: 10 Minutes
Cook Time: 15 Minutes
Serves: 6

Ingredients:

- 2 lbs of ground beef
- ½ lb of ground pork
- 2 eggs at room temperature
- 1 tablespoon of almond flour
- 1 green onion finely chopped
- 1 tablespoon of oregano
- 2 tablespoons of fresh parsley finely chopped
- 1 teaspoon of cumin
- 3 tablespoons of olive oil
- Salt and ground pepper to taste

Directions:

1. IIn a deep bowl or container, combine all ingredients from the list above.
2. IUsing your hands knead the meat mixture until combine well.
3. IWet your hands with water, then form the meat into small meatballs.
4. IPlace your meatballs in Air fryer basket in a single layer.
5. ICook on 380 F for 12 to 13 minutes or until internal temperature reaches a temperature of 165 degrees.
6. IRepeat with all remaining meatballs.
7. IServe hot and enjoy!

Nutritional Value (Amount per Serving):

Calories: 554; Fat: 34.96; Carb: 3.73; Protein: 53.58

Air Fryer Sirloin Steaks with Garlic Butter

Prep Time: 10 Minutes
Cook Time: 10 Minutes
Serves: 4

Ingredients:

- 2 Sirloin Steaks, about 1 inch thick
- 2 tablespoons olive oil
- 1 teaspoon salt
- 1/2 teaspoon black pepper
- 4 tablespoons room temperature butter, unsalted
- 1 tablespoon diced fresh parsley
- 1 tablespoon dried fresh chives
- 1 teaspoon minced garlic
- 1/8 teaspoon crushed red pepper flakes

Directions:

1. IStart by taking out the meat and letting it set to room temperature, about 20 to 30 minutes. This will help your steak cook more evenly.
2. IThen preheat your air fryer to 400 degrees F, air fryer setting, for 5 minutes. Rub the olive oil over the steak, and then season your steak with salt and pepper.
3. IAdd your steak. The guide is: 10 minutes for medium-rare, 12 minutes for medium, 14 minutes for medium-well (but it will depend on your air fryer and how thick your steak is. So, use a meat thermometer for best results).
4. IMake the Garlic Butter: In a small bowl, mash the butter, minced garlic, and fresh herbs together.
5. IAdd some garlic butter on top of your cooked steak.
6. IPlate, serve, and enjoy!

Nutritional Value (Amount per Serving):

Calories: 439; Fat: 24.77; Carb: 0.58; Protein: 50.76

Air Fried Ajo Pork Side Ribs

Prep Time: 10 Minutes
Cook Time: 20 Minutes
Serves: 6

Ingredients:

- 3 lbs of pork side ribs
- ⅓ cup of garlic-infused olive oil
- 4 tablespoons of ketchup (keto)
- 1 teaspoon of garlic powder
- 3 tablespoons chives finely chopped
- Salt and black pepper to taste

Directions:

1. ICut pork into individual ribs to fit your Air fryer basket; place into a container.
2. IIn a bowl, stir together the olive oil, garlic powder, chives, ketchup, and the salt and pepper.
3. IRub generously your ribs with the garlic mixture.
4. IPlace seasoned ribs into your Air fryer basket.
5. ICook on 400 F for 20 to 22 minutes.
6. IAllow resting 15 minutes before serving.
7. IEnjoy!

Nutritional Value (Amount per Serving):

Calories: 380; Fat: 17.94; Carb: 4.26; Protein: 47.53

Air-Fryer Pork Tenderloin

Prep Time: 10 Minutes
Cook Time: 20 Minutes
Serves: 4

Ingredients:

- 1 tablespoon brown sugar
- 2 teaspoons Dijon mustard
- 1 teaspoon balsamic vinegar
- ½ teaspoon garlic powder
- ½ teaspoon onion powder
- ½ teaspoon smoked paprika
- ½ teaspoon salt
- ¼ teaspoon ground pepper
- 1 pound pork tenderloin, trimmed

Directions:

1. IPreheat air fryer to 400°F for 5 minutes.
2. IWhisk brown sugar, mustard, vinegar, garlic powder, onion powder, paprika, salt and pepper together in a small bowl.
3. IPat pork dry with paper towels. (If using a small air fryer, cut the pork in half crosswise.) Rub the spice mixture onto the pork and place in the fryer basket. Cook until an instant-read thermometer inserted in the thickest part registers 145°F, 15 to 18 minutes. Let rest for 5 minutes before slicing.

Nutritional Value (Amount per Serving):

Calories: 177; Fat: 4.11; Carb: 3.32; Protein: 29.97

Air Fryer Beef Roast With Mustard

Prep Time: 20 Minutes
Cook Time: 35 Minutes
Serves: 8

Ingredients:

- 4 lb of beef roast, grass-fed, boneless
- Salt and ground pepper to taste
- 2 tablespoons of a mustard grain
- 1 tablespoon of fresh lemon juice freshly squeezed
- 2 teaspoons of dried basil, crushed
- 2 teaspoons of fresh rosemary finely chopped
- 2 tablespoons of water
- 1 to 2 tablespoons of ghee softened

Directions:

1. IPreheat the air fryer to 360 F.
2. ISeason generously meat with the salt and pepper.
3. IIn a separate bowl, combine all remaining ingredients, and rub in meat.
4. IPlace beef roast in the air fryer basket, and cook for 45 to 48 minutes for medium-rare (turn meat after 20 minutes).
5. IRemove beef from the air fryer, and leave to rest for 10 to 15 minutes before serving.
6. ISlice and serve.

Nutritional Value (Amount per Serving):

Calories: 422; Fat: 19.93; Carb: 1.24; Protein: 60.81

Perfect Air Fried Pork Burgers

Prep Time: 10 Minutes
Cook Time: 25 Minutes
Serves: 4

Ingredients:

- 2 lb of ground pork
- 1 spring onion finely chopped
- ½ teaspoon of garlic powder
- 1 tablespoon of fresh sage, chopped
- ½ teaspoon of cumin
- ⅓ teaspoon of cayenne pepper (or to taste)
- ½ teaspoon of fennel seeds (optional)
- Salt and pepper to taste

Directions:

1. IPreheat the air fryer to 350F.
2. IIn a bowl or container, combine ground pork with all remaining ingredients.
3. IUse hands to mix the mixture thoroughly.
4. IForm mixture into 8 burgers/patties.
5. IPlace the hamburgers on the racks.
6. IPlace burgers into Air fryer basket 4 at the time.
7. ICook for 12 to 13 minutes; flip the burger halfway through cooking.
8. IServe hot.

Nutritional Value (Amount per Serving):

Calories: 685; Fat: 47.33; Carb: 2.27; Protein: 58.78

Air Fryer Coconut Marinated Flank Steak

Prep Time: 10 Minutes
Cook Time: 20 Minutes
Serves: 6

Ingredients:

- 4 tablespoons coconut oil, melted
- ¾ cup of coconut aminos
- 2 teaspoons of black pepper
- 1 teaspoon of ground turmeric
- 1 teaspoon of fresh ginger
- 4 lbs flank steak

Directions:

1. IIn a deep baking dish, combine all ingredients (except the flank steak).
2. IPlace steak into a deep container and coat with marinade; cover and place in refrigerator to marinate overnight.
3. IPreheat the Air Fryer at 400 F (for 3 minutes).
4. ICook for about 25 minutes.
5. IRemove from the Air Fryer basket and let it rest for 10 minutes.
6. ISlice and serve.

Nutritional Value (Amount per Serving):

Calories: 502; Fat: 24.3; Carb: 2.13; Protein: 65.18

Air Fryer Lamb Chops With Fresh Herbs

Prep Time: 20 Minutes
Cook Time: 50 Minutes
Serves: 6

Ingredients:

- 3 lbs. of lamb chops
- Salt and ground pepper to taste
- 2 tablespoons of garlic-infused olive oil
- 2 to 3 cloves minced garlic
- 3 teaspoons of fresh basil leaves, finely chopped
- 3 teaspoons fresh parsley leaves, finely chopped
- 3 teaspoons fresh thyme leaves, finely chopped

Directions:

1. ISeason the lamb chops with the salt and pepper.
2. IIn a container, combine minced garlic, fresh herbs, and olive oil; rub the herb mixture on both sides of the lamb chops.
3. ICover and refrigerate for at least 2 hours.
4. IRemove from refrigerator and allow the chops to come to room temperature.
5. IPreheat your Air Fryer to 360 F/ (for 3 minutes).
6. IPlace the lamb chops onto the air fryer grill pan.
7. ICook the lamb chops for 6 to 7 minutes per side.
8. ILeave it to rest for 5 minutes and serve.

Nutritional Value (Amount per Serving):

Calories: 748; Fat: 64.93; Carb: 1.18; Protein: 34.28

Air Fryer Steak In Sour Marinade

Prep Time: 10 Minutes
Cook Time: 25 Minutes
Serves: 5

Ingredients:

- 2 tablespoons of fresh lavender finely chopped
- ½ teaspoon of chopped fresh thyme
- Kosher salt and freshly ground black pepper
- ½ cup of apple cider vinegar (preferably non-pasteurized)
- ½ cup of olive oil
- 2 ½ lbs of rib-eye steak boneless

Directions:

1. ICombine lavender with thyme, olive oil, vinegar, salt, and pepper.
2. IPlace steak in a large container and pour the mixture.
3. ICover, and marinate the steak for at least 4 hours in refrigerator.
4. IPreheat the Air Fryer at 400 F (for 3 minutes)
5. IPlace a marinated steak in the Air Fryer Basket, and cook for 25 minutes.
6. ILet it rest 10 minutes before slicing and serving.

Nutritional Value (Amount per Serving):

Calories: 701; Fat: 47.86; Carb: 2.82; Protein: 67.74

Garlic-Paprika Marinated Pork Chops (Air Fryer)

Prep Time: 25 Minutes
Cook Time: 30 Minutes
Serves: 6

Ingredients:

- 3 lbs of pork chops bone-in (or boneless)
- 3 cloves of garlic minced
- 1 tablespoon of paprika
- 2 to 3 tablespoon of olive oil (or lard melted)
- ½ cup of fresh lemon juice
- 1 teaspoon of dry onion powder
- 1 teaspoon of ground mustard
- Kosher salt and fresh ground black pepper to taste

Directions:

1. IIn a container, combine all ingredients except pork chops.
2. IAdd pork chops, cover and toss to combine well.
3. IRefrigerate for 4 hours; remove pork from marinade and pat with kitchen paper towel.
4. IPreheat air fryer to 400 F (for 5 minutes).
5. ICook pork chops in air fryer basket for 12 to 14 minutes, flipping pork chops over after 6 to 7 minutes.
6. IServe hot or warm. Enjoy!

Nutritional Value (Amount per Serving):

Calories: 530; Fat: 29.93; Carb: 3.63; Protein: 58.69

Air-Fryer Buffalo Wings

Prep Time: 10 Minutes
Cook Time: 60 Minutes
Serves: 4

Ingredients:

- 1 ½ teaspoons paprika
- ½ teaspoon garlic powder
- ½ teaspoon onion powder
- ½ teaspoon ground pepper
- 3 ½ to 4 pounds chicken wings, separated if necessary
- ½ cup Buffalo-style hot sauce (such as Frank›s RedHot)
- 2 tablespoons unsalted butter
- ¼ cup ranch dressing
- 2 carrots, cut into sticks
- 1 stalk celery, cut into sticks

Directions:

1. IPreheat oven to 200 degrees F. Preheat air fryer to 375 degrees F. Combine paprika, garlic powder, onion powder and pepper in a large bowl. Add wings and toss to coat. Let stand for 10 minutes.
2. IAdd half of the wings to the air-fryer basket; cook for 15 minutes. Turn the wings; continue to cook until they're crispy and a thermometer inserted in the thickest portion registers 165 degrees F, about 5 minutes. Arrange the wings in a single layer on a baking sheet; transfer to the oven to keep warm. Repeat the process with the remaining wings.
3. ICook hot sauce and butter in a small saucepan over medium-high heat, whisking often, until the butter melts and the mixture is smooth, 2 to 3 minutes.
4. ITransfer the wings to a large bowl. Add the butter sauce and toss to coat. Serve alongside ranch dressing, carrots and celery.

Nutritional Value (Amount per Serving):

Calories: 1298; Fat: 84.85; Carb: 51.64; Protein: 77.66

Air Fryer Flank Steak with Homemade Chimichurri Sauce

Prep Time: 10 Minutes
Cook Time: 20 Minutes
Serves: 4

Ingredients:

- 2 pounds flank steak
- 1/2 cup diced parsley
- 1/2 cup diced cilantro
- 1/2 onion
- 1 teaspoon kosher salt
- 1/2 teaspoon black pepper
- 1 teaspoon garlic
- 1/2 teaspoon red pepper flakes
- 1/3 cup olive oil
- 2 tablespoons red wine vinegar

Directions:

1. ILet the flank steak get to room temperature, which will be about 15 to 30 minutes.
Preheat your air fryer to 400 degrees F, air fryer setting, for about 5 minutes.
2. IRub the olive oil or butter all over the steak, and season with salt and pepper.
3. ISet the steaks in the air fryer for 15-20 minutes, flipping halfway.
4. IRemove the steak, and let it rest for about 5 minutes before slicing.
5. ICheck the internal temperature of the steak, which should be 135 degrees F.
6. IPlate, serve, and enjoy!

Nutritional Value (Amount per Serving):

Calories: 229; Fat: 20.09; Carb: 2.35; Protein: 9.78

Air Fryer Beef Tenderloin

Prep Time: 5 Minutes
Cook Time: 35 Minutes
Serves: 8

Ingredients:

- 2 pounds beef tenderloin, at room temperature
- 1 tablespoon vegetable oil
- 1 teaspoon dried oregano
- 1 teaspoon salt
- ½ teaspoon cracked black pepper

Directions:

1. IPreheat the air fryer to 400 degrees F.
2. IPat dry tenderloin with paper towels and place on a plate. Drizzle oil all over meat, then sprinkle with oregano, salt, and pepper. Rub spices and oil into meat. Place into the preheated air fryer basket, folding as needed to make it fit. Close the lid.
3. IReduce heat to 390 degrees F and cook for 22 minutes. Reduce heat to 360 degrees F and cook for 10 more minutes. An instant-read thermometer inserted into the center of tenderloin should read 135 degrees F for medium doneness.
4. IRemove tenderloin to a platter. Allow to rest, uncovered, for at least 10 minutes before serving.

Nutritional Value (Amount per Serving):

Calories: 255; Fat: 11.82; Carb: 0.21; Protein: 34.62

Air Fryer Corned Beef Hash

Prep Time: 15 Minutes
Cook Time: 25 Minutes
Serves: 2

Ingredients:

- 1 pound red potatoes, cubed
- ½ cup chopped green bell pepper
- ½ cup chopped onion
- 2 teaspoons vegetable oil
- ½ teaspoon paprika
- salt and ground black pepper to taste
- 1 cup cubed leftover corned beef
- 2 eggs

Directions:

1. IPreheat an air fryer to 400 degrees F.
2. ICombine potatoes, bell pepper, and onion in a large bowl. Add vegetable oil, paprika, salt, and pepper. Stir until potatoes are evenly coated. Transfer mixture to the basket of the air fryer.
3. ICook for 10 minutes. Shake and cook for 5 more minutes. Stir in the corned beef and cook for 5 minutes.
4. IMake 2 small wells in the mixture. Crack 1 egg into each well. Cook until eggs are set and cooked to desired doneness, about 3 minutes.

Nutritional Value (Amount per Serving):

Calories: 421; Fat: 17.49; Carb: 43.28; Protein: 24.59

Chapter 5:
Fish and Seafood

Air Fryer Salmon Patties

Prep Time: 10 Minutes
Cook Time: 10 Minutes
Serves: 4

Ingredients:

- 1 ½ lb of salmon fillets, skin and bones removed, cut into small cubes
- 2 tablespoons of sesame seeds toasted
- 2 large eggs at room temperature
- 1 tablespoon of Extra Virgin Olive Oil
- 1 tablespoon of lemon juice freshly squeezed
- 2 cloves of garlic finely chopped
- 1 teaspoon of fresh ginger, peeled and grated
- 1 cup of green onions, chopped
- 1 tablespoon of almond flour

Directions:

1. IPreheat your air fryer to 365 F.
2. IIn a bowl, combine together the salmon fillets with all remaining ingredients.
3. IMix until all ingredients combine well.
4. IDivide the mixture into 6 equal portions and make patties.
5. IAdd patties to the air fryer basket in a single layer.
6. ICook for 7 to 8 minutes; turn the patties half a way through the cooking time.
7. IServe immediately.

Nutritional Value (Amount per Serving):

Calories: 452; Fat: 27.57; Carb: 2.71; Protein: 49.14

Air-Fryer Fish Tacos

Prep Time: 10 Minutes
Cook Time: 20 Minutes
Serves: 4

Ingredients:

- 2 cups shredded green cabbage
- ¼ cup coarsely chopped fresh cilantro
- 1 scallion, thinly sliced
- 5 tablespoons lime juice (from 2 limes), divided
- 1 tablespoon avocado oil
- 1 large avocado
- 2 tablespoons sour cream
- 1 small clove garlic, grated
- ¼ teaspoon salt
- 1 large egg white
- ⅓ cup dry whole-wheat breadcrumbs
- 1 tablespoon chili powder
- 1 pound skinless mahi-mahi fillets, cut into 2- to 3-inch strips
- Avocado oil cooking spray
- 8 (6 inch) corn tortillas, warmed
- 1 medium tomato, chopped

Directions:

1. IToss cabbage, cilantro, scallion, 2 tablespoons lime juice and avocado oil together in a medium bowl; set aside.
2. ICut avocado in half lengthwise; using a spoon, scoop the pulp into the bowl of a mini food processor. Add sour cream, garlic, salt and the remaining 3 tablespoons lime juice; process until smooth, about 30 seconds. (Alternatively, mash with a fork to reach desired consistency.) Set aside.
3. IPreheat air fryer to 400°F. Place egg white in a shallow dish; whisk until frothy. Combine breadcrumbs and chili powder in a separate shallow dish. Pat fish dry with a paper towel. Coat the fish with egg white, letting excess drip off; dredge in the breadcrumb mixture, pressing to adhere.

4. IWorking in batches if needed, arrange the fish in an even layer in the fryer basket; coat the fish well with cooking spray. Cook until crispy and golden on one side, about 3 minutes. Flip the fish; coat with cooking spray and cook until it's crispy and flakes easily, about 3 minutes. Flake the fish into bite-size pieces. Top each tortilla evenly with fish, avocado crema (about 1 tablespoon each), cabbage slaw (about 1/4 cup each) and tomato. Serve with lime wedges, if desired.

Nutritional Value (Amount per Serving):

Calories: 1223; Fat: 44.38; Carb: 167.16; Protein: 47.52

Air-Fryer Tilapia

Prep Time: 10 Minutes
Cook Time: 15 Minutes
Serves: 4

Ingredients:

- Cooking spray
- 1 ¼ pounds tilapia fillets
- 1 teaspoon grated lemon zest
- ¼ teaspoon garlic powder
- ¼ teaspoon onion powder
- ¼ teaspoon salt, divided
- ⅛ teaspoon hot paprika
- ⅛ teaspoon ground white pepper
- 1 tablespoon lemon juice
- 1 teaspoon chopped fresh chives
- 1 teaspoon chopped fresh parsley

Directions:

1. IPreheat air fryer to 400°F for 5 minutes. Lightly coat the fryer basket with cooking spray.
2. IPat tilapia fillets dry with paper towels. Coat the fillets with cooking spray.
3. ICombine lemon zest, garlic powder, onion powder, 1/8 teaspoon salt, paprika and white pepper in a small bowl. Sprinkle onto the fish.
4. IWorking in batches if necessary, arrange the fish in a single layer in the fryer basket. Cook, flipping once, until an instant-read thermometer inserted in the center registers 145°F and the fish flakes easily with a fork at the thickest part, 6 to 8 minutes. Drizzle lemon juice over the fillets and sprinkle with the remaining 1/8 teaspoon salt. Sprinkle with chives and parsley before serving.

Nutritional Value (Amount per Serving):

Calories: 139; Fat: 2.44; Carb: 0.83; Protein: 28.59

Air-Fryer Tuna Steak

Prep Time: 10 Minutes
Cook Time: 20 Minutes
Serves: 4

Ingredients:

- 3 tablespoons lower-sodium tamari or soy sauce
- 1 scallion, thinly sliced
- 1 tablespoon lime juice
- 2 teaspoons sesame oil
- 2 teaspoons honey
- 1 clove garlic, minced
- 2 tablespoons toasted sesame seeds
- 2 (8 ounce) ahi tuna steaks (1 inch thick)

Directions:

1. ICombine tamari (or soy sauce), scallion, lime juice, sesame oil, honey and garlic in a small bowl; set aside.
2. ISpread sesame seeds on a small plate. Coat both sides of each tuna steak evenly with sesame seeds, pressing to adhere.
3. IPreheat air fryer to 375°F. Place the tuna steaks in the fryer basket and cook to desired doneness (about 7 minutes for medium-rare or 10 minutes for medium). Slice the tuna steaks and drizzle evenly with the reserved sauce.

Nutritional Value (Amount per Serving):

Calories: 264; Fat: 11.5; Carb: 5.26; Protein: 33.97

Simple Air Fried Shrimp With Paprika

Prep Time: 10 Minutes
Cook Time: 15 Minutes
Serves: 4

Ingredients:

- 2 lb of fresh shrimps
- 3 tablespoons of olive oil
- 1 tablespoon of sweet paprika powder
- Sea-salt flakes

Directions:

1. IPreheat your Air fryer to 380 F.
2. IIn a large bowl add shrimp and sprinkle with olive oil, paprika and season with the salt.
3. IStir gently with your hands to combine well.
4. IPlace 4 to 5 shrimp in the basket (in a single layer) and cook for 5 minutes.
5. IRepeat until all shrimp are cooked.
6. IServe hot.

Nutritional Value (Amount per Serving):

Calories: 321; Fat: 13.43; Carb: 0.92; Protein: 46.55

Air Fryer Lemony Marinated Sardine

Prep Time: 20 Minutes
Cook Time: 50 Minutes
Serves: 4

Ingredients:

- 2 lbs of sardines, cleaned
- Salt to taste
- 1 tablespoon of fresh oregano
- ¼ cup of lemon juice, freshly squeezed
- ¼ cup of olive oil
- 1 lemon, sliced

Directions:

1. IIn a container, whisk lemon juice, oil olive, oregano, and salt.
2. IAdd sardine and toss to combine well.
3. ICover and marinate in the fridge for 4 hours.
4. ITake your sardines out of the marinade, rinse under cold water and pat dry on a kitchen paper towel.
5. IPut into the air fryer pan.
6. ICook at 380F for 15 minutes.
7. ISprinkle with olive oil and lemon juice and serve.

Nutritional Value (Amount per Serving):

Calories: 607; Fat: 39.69; Carb: 4.46; Protein: 56.27

Air Fryer Keto Almond Crusted Salmon

Prep Time: 10 Minutes
Cook Time: 10 Minutes
Serves: 4

Ingredients:

- 1 ¼ lb of salmon filet, skinless
- 2 teaspoons of paprika
- 1 cup of almond flour or almond meal
- Salt and ground black pepper to taste
- 3 tablespoons of olive oil

Directions:

1. IIn a bowl, combine together the almond meal, paprika, salt, and pepper.
2. ICut the salmon into even-sized long strips.
3. ISprinkle each piece of salmon with olive oil, and then roll evenly into the almond mixture.
4. IPlace breaded salmon fillets in the basket of the air fryer.
5. ICook fish on 400 F for 6 to 7 minutes.
6. IServe immediately.

Nutritional Value (Amount per Serving):

Calories: 714; Fat: 27.09; Carb: 29.26; Protein: 90.2

Air Fryer Spiced Shrimp

Prep Time: 10 Minutes
Cook Time: 10 Minutes
Serves: 4

Ingredients:

- 2 lbs of shrimp cleaned
- 1 tablespoon of fresh ginger grated
- Salt and black pepper to taste
- 1 tablespoon of cumin seeds
- ¼ teaspoon of turmeric
- ¼ teaspoon of cinnamon (optional)
- ¼ teaspoon of cayenne pepper
- ½ cup of sesame oil (or olive oil)
- 2 tablespoons of lemon juice
- Lemon slices for serving

Directions:

1. IIn a large container, combine all spices, sesame oil, and the lemon juice.
2. IAdd shrimp, cover and toss to combine well; refrigerate for 30 minutes.
3. IAdd shrimp to air fryer basket in a single layer.
4. ICook at 400 F for about 10-14 minutes; shake and flip halfway.
5. ITransfer shrimp on a serving plate.
6. ISprinkle with the fresh lemon juice and serve with lemon slices.

Nutritional Value (Amount per Serving):

Calories: 485; Fat: 30.78; Carb: 3.69; Protein: 46.94

Keto Breaded Tilapia Fish Sticks (Air Fryer)

Prep Time: 10 Minutes
Cook Time: 20 Minutes
Serves: 4

Ingredients:

- Cooking spray
- 2 tilapia fish fillets cut into strips
- ½ cup of almond flour
- 2 tablespoons of grated Romano or Parmesan cheese
- 1 teaspoon of garlic powder
- 1 teaspoon dried parsley
- 2 eggs beaten
- Salt and ground black pepper to taste

Directions:

1. IPreheat your Air Fryer at 400 F.
2. IGrease the bottom of your air fryer basket with cooking spray.
3. ICut fish in into strips the size of a finger; season with the salt to taste.
4. IIn a bowl combine together almond flour with cheese, garlic powder and parsley.
5. IIn a separate bowl, whisk the eggs with a pinch of salt and pepper.
6. IDip the fish into the egg mixture and then, roll fish fingers in almond-cheese mixture.
7. IPlace the fish fillets in the Air Fryer basket and cook for 10 minutes.
8. IFlip the fish and grease with cooking spray; cook for an additional 7 minutes.

Serve hot or cold.

Nutritional Value (Amount per Serving):

Calories: 175; Fat: 10.92; Carb: 2.54; Protein: 15.94

Air-Fryer Tuna Patties

Prep Time: 20 Minutes
Cook Time: 30 Minutes
Serves: 4

Ingredients:

- 2 (5 ounce) cans solid white tuna in water, drained and flaked
- ¾ cup whole-wheat panko
- ¼ cup finely chopped red onion
- ¼ cup finely chopped red bell pepper
- ¼ cup finely chopped celery
- 1 large egg, lightly beaten
- 7 tablespoons mayonnaise, divided
- 3 tablespoons chopped fresh flat-leaf parsley, divided
- 1 ½ teaspoons grated lemon zest, divided
- 2 tablespoons lemon juice, divided
- Cooking spray
- 1 tablespoon Dijon mustard
- 4 cups arugula (about 4 ounces)

Directions:

1. IPlace tuna, panko, onion, bell pepper, celery, egg, 4 tablespoons mayonnaise, 2 tablespoons parsley, 1 teaspoon lemon zest and 1 tablespoon lemon juice in a medium bowl. Stir gently to combine. Shape the mixture into 8 patties 2 1/2 inches in diameter and about 1/2 inch thick (about 1/3 cup mixture per patty). Place the patties on a parchment-paper-lined plate and refrigerate for 20 minutes.
2. IMeanwhile, preheat an air fryer to 360°F for 15 minutes. Lightly coat the fry basket with cooking spray and coat each patty with cooking spray. Working in batches if needed, add the patties to the basket in a single layer; cook until slightly crisp and heated through, about 6 minutes per side. (Lightly coat the basket with cooking spray between batches.)
3. IMeanwhile, combine mustard and the remaining 3 tablespoons mayonnaise, 1 tablespoon parsley, 1/2 teaspoon lemon zest and 1

tablespoon lemon juice in a small bowl; stir until smooth. Place 2 tuna patties, 1 cup arugula and 1 tablespoon mayonnaise sauce on each of 4 plates.

Nutritional Value (Amount per Serving):

Calories: 257; Fat: 12.52; Carb: 10.97; Protein: 25.09

Air Fryer Salmon Cakes

Prep Time: 35 Minutes
Cook Time: 15 Minutes
Serves: 4

Ingredients:

- 1 lb Fresh Atlantic Salmon Side (half a side)
- 1/4 Cup Avocado, mashed
- 1/4 Cup Cilantro, diced + additional for garnish
- 1 1/2 tsp Yellow curry powder
- 1/2 tsp Stonemill Sea Salt Grinder
- 1/4 Cup + 4 tsp Tapioca Starch, divided
- 2 Organic Cage Free Brown Eggs
- 1/2 Cup Organic Coconut Flakes
- Organic Coconut Oil, melted (for brushing)
- 2 tsp Organic Coconut Oil, melted
- 6 Cups Organic Arugula & Spinach Mix, tightly packed
- Pinch of Stonemill Sea Salt Grinder

Directions:

1. IRemove the skin from the salmon, dice the flesh, and add it into a large bowl.
2. IAdd in the avocado, cilantro, curry powder, sea salt and stir until well mixed. Then, stir in 4 tsp of the tapioca starch until well incorporated.
3. ILine a baking sheet with parchment paper. Form the salmon into 8, 1/4 cup-sized patties, just over 1/2 inch thick, and place them onto the pan. Freeze for 20 minutes so they are easier to work with.
4. IWhile the patties freeze, pre-heat your Air Fryer to 400 degrees for 10 minutes, rubbing the basket with coconut oil. Additionally, whisk the eggs and place them into a shallow plate. Place the remaining 1/4 cup of Tapioca starch and the coconut flakes in separate shallow plates as well.
5. IOnce the patties have chilled, dip one into the tapioca starch, making sure it's fully covered. Then, dip it into the egg, covering it entirely, and gently brushing off any excess. Finally, press just the top and sides of the cake

into the coconut flakes and place it, coconut flake-side up, into the air fryer. Repeat with all cakes.

6. IGently brush the tops with a little bit of melted coconut oil (optional, but recommended) and cook until the outside is golden brown and crispy, and the inside is juicy and tender, about 15 minutes. Note: the patties will stick to the Air Fryer basked a little, so use a sharp-edged spatula to remove them.

7. IWhen the cakes have about 5 minutes left to cook, heat the coconut oil up in a large pan on medium heat. Add in the Arugula and Spinach Mix, and a pinch of salt, and cook, stirring constantly, until the greens JUST begin to wilt, only 30 seconds – 1 minute.

8. IDivide the greens between 4 plates, followed by the salmon cakes. Garnish with extra cilantro and DEVOUR!

Nutritional Value (Amount per Serving):

Calories: 419; Fat: 20.32; Carb: 26.61; Protein: 36.67

Air Fryer Parmesan Shrimp

Prep Time: 10 Minutes
Cook Time: 10 Minutes
Serves: 4

Ingredients:

- 2 pounds jumbo cooked shrimp, peeled and deveined
- 4 cloves garlic, minced
- 2/3 cup parmesan cheese, grated
- 1 teaspoon pepper
- 1/2 teaspoon oregano
- 1 teaspoon basil
- 1 teaspoon onion powder
- 2 tablespoons olive oil
- Lemon, quartered

Directions:

1. IIn a large bowl, combine garlic, parmesan cheese, pepper, oregano, basil, onion powder and olive oil.
2. IGently toss shrimp in mixture until evenly-coated.
3. ISpray air fryer basket with non-stick spray and place shrimp in basket.
4. ICook at 350 degrees for 8-10 minutes or until seasoning on shrimp is browned.
5. ISqueeze the lemon over the shrimps before serving.

Nutritional Value (Amount per Serving):

Calories: 371; Fat: 14.58; Carb: 5.79; Protein: 51.63

Air Fryer Lemon and Herb Tilapia

Prep Time: 5 Minutes
Cook Time: 10 Minutes
Serves: 4

Ingredients:

- 1 teaspoon lemon juice
- 1 teaspoon dried oregano
- 1 teaspoon garlic powder
- 1 teaspoon salt
- 4 tilapia fillets about 6 ounces

Directions:

1. IStart by making the rub, mix the lemon juice, oregano, garlic powder, and salt.
2. IThen rub the spices onto the fish. (Both sides)
3. ISpray the fish with olive oil spray, and then place it into the air fryer basket or oven. Set the temperature to 400 degrees F for 4 minutes. After 4 minutes, flip (spray again) and add another 4 minutes.
4. IPlate, serve, and enjoy!

Nutritional Value (Amount per Serving):

Calories: 115; Fat: 1.99; Carb: 0.82; Protein: 23.45

Keto Air Fryer Fish Sticks

Prep Time: 10 Minutes
Cook Time: 10 Minutes
Serves: 4

Ingredients:

- 1 lb white fish such as cod
- ¼ cup mayonnaise
- 2 tablespoons Dijon mustard
- 2 tablespoons water
- 1 ½ cups pork rind panko such as Pork King Good
- ¾ teaspoon cajun seasoning
- Salt and pepper to taste

Directions:

1. ISpray the air fryer rack with non-stick cooking spray (I use avocado oil spray).
2. IPat the fish dry and cut into sticks about 1 inch by 2 inches wide (how you are able to cut it will depend a little on what kind of fish you buy and how thick and wide it is).
3. IIn a small shallow bowl, whisk together the mayo, mustard, and water. In another shallow bowl, whisk together the pork rinds and Cajun seasoning. Add salt and pepper to taste (both the pork rinds and seasoning could have a fair bit of salt, so dip a finger in to taste how salty it is).
4. IWorking with one piece of fish at a time, dip into the mayo mixture to coat and then tap off the excess. Dip into the pork rind mixture and toss to coat. Place on the air fryer rack.
5. ISet to Air Fry at 400F and bake 5 minutes, then flip the fish sticks with tongs and bake another 5 minutes. Serve immediately.

Nutritional Value (Amount per Serving):

Calories: 231; Fat: 9.88; Carb: 12.64; Protein: 23.02

Chapter 6: Vegetarian

Air Fryer Artichokes With Feta Yogurt Dip

Prep Time: 15 Minutes
Cook Time: 15 Minutes
Serves: 4

Ingredients:

- 2 large artichokes, trimmed and cut in half
- 1 small lemon, cut into quarters
- 1 tablespoon extra-virgin olive oil
- Fine salt and black pepper
- ⅓ cup plain Greek yogurt
- ¼ cup crumbled feta cheese
- Zest and juice of 1 small lemon (about 1 tablespoon zest and 2 tablespoons juice)
- 1 tablespoon extra-virgin olive oil
- 1 tablespoon dairy or unsweetened non-dairy milk
- 1 garlic clove, grated or minced
- 1 tablespoon finely chopped fresh dill (or 1 teaspoon dried dill)
- 1 tablespoon finely chopped fresh mint (or 1 teaspoon dried mint)
- ¼ teaspoon fine salt, plus more to taste
- ¼ teaspoon ground black pepper

Directions:

1. IPreheat the air fryer to 350°F.
2. IPrepare the artichokes by pulling off the outer leaves from the bottom of the artichoke.
3. IUsing a large knife, cut off the bottom of the stem and the top ⅓ of each artichoke.
4. IUsing scissors or kitchen shears, snip the pointy end off of each leaf (if you're not using globe artichokes, which have rounded leaf tips). Then, slice each artichoke in half.
5. IRemove the fuzzy choke in the middle of each artichoke half. To do this, use a spoon to scrape out the fuzzy parts, leaving the leaves and heart

intact. Rub all cut sides of the artichoke with the quartered lemon pieces to prevent browning.

6. IDrizzle the cut sides of the artichokes with olive oil, and rub the oil over the entire artichoke. Sprinkle with salt and pepper.

7. IPlace the artichokes, cut side down, into the basket of the air fryer. Air fry for 12-15 minutes total, flipping them over halfway. You'll know the artichokes are done when a leaf can be easily pulled from the base of the artichoke and you can easily pierce the heart with the tip of a paring knife.

8. IWhile the artichokes cook, make the dip. In a bowl, combine the Greek yogurt, feta cheese, lemon juice and zest, olive oil, milk, garlic, dill, mint, salt, and pepper. Taste and adjust salt and pepper as needed. Refrigerate until ready to serve. Leftover dip may be stored in an airtight container in the refrigerator for up to 4 days.

Nutritional Value (Amount per Serving):

Calories: 111; Fat: 5055; Carb: 13.52; Protein: 5.13

Air Fryer Roasted Asian Broccoli

Prep Time: 10 Minutes
Cook Time: 20 Minutes
Serves: 4

Ingredients:

- 1 Lb Broccoli, Cut into florets
- 1 1/2 Tbsp Peanut oil
- 1 Tbsp Garlic, minced
- Salt
- 2 Tbsp Reduced sodium soy sauce
- 2 tsp Honey (or agave)
- 2 tsp Sriracha
- 1 tsp Rice vinegar
- 1/3 Cup Roasted salted peanuts
- Fresh lime juice (optional)

Directions:

1. IIn a large bowl, toss together the broccoli, peanut oil, garlic and season with sea salt. Make sure the oil covers all the broccoli florets. I like to use my hands to give each one a quick rub.
2. ISpread the broccoli into the wire basket of your air fryer, in a single layer as much as possible, trying to leave a little bit of space between each floret.
3. ICook at 400 degrees until golden brown and crispy, about 15 – 20 minutes, stirring halfway.
4. IWhile the broccoli cook, mix together the honey, soy sauce, sriracha and rice vinegar in a small, microwave-safe bowl.
5. IOnce mixed, microwave the mixture for 10-15 seconds until the honey is melted, and evenly incorporated.
6. ITransfer the cooked broccoli to a bowl, and add in the soy sauce mixture. Toss to coat and season to taste with a pinch more salt, if needed.
7. IStir in the peanuts and squeeze lime on top (if desired.)

Nutritional Value (Amount per Serving):

Calories: 157; Fat: 10.36; Carb: 12.92; Protein: 6.36

Air-Fryer Cabbage

Prep Time: 20 Minutes
Cook Time: 35 Minutes
Serves: 8

Ingredients:

- 1 small head red or green cabbage (about 2 pounds)
- 2 tablespoons extra-virgin olive oil
- 6 tablespoons grated Parmesan cheese
- 1 teaspoon garlic powder
- 1 teaspoon onion powder
- ½ teaspoon salt
- ½ teaspoon ground pepper

Directions:

1. IPreheat air fryer to 350°F for 5 minutes. Cut cabbage into 8 (2-inch) wedges, keeping core intact. Brush the wedges with oil on both sides.
2. IMix Parmesan, garlic powder, onion powder, salt and pepper together in a small bowl. Spoon the mixture onto 1 side of each cabbage wedge, coaxing the mixture into the grooves to help it adhere. Working in batches if necessary, arrange the wedges in the fryer basket in a single layer, Parmesan-sides up.
3. ICook until slightly browned on the outside and tender in the middle, about 25 minutes.

Nutritional Value (Amount per Serving):

Calories: 55; Fat: 2.67; Carb: 6.53; Protein: 2.24

Air Fryer Brussels Sprouts With Chipotle-Lime Aioli

Prep Time: 10 Minutes
Cook Time: 15 Minutes
Serves: 4-6

Ingredients:

- 1 lb Brussels sprouts
- 1 tablespoon olive oil or avocado oil
- 1/2 teaspoon coarse sea salt
- 1/3 cup mayonnaise
- 1/2 teaspoon grated lime zest (1/2 lime)
- 1 teaspoon fresh lime juice
- 1 garlic clove, grated or finely minced
- 1/8 teaspoon chipotle powder 1/8 teaspoon smoked paprika
- Pinch of coarse sea salt

Directions:

1. ISet the air fryer to 375 degrees and allow it to preheat.
2. ITrim the stem ends from the Brussels sprouts and cut each Brussel into quarters (cut very small Brussels only in half). Save any loose Brussels sprout leaves (you can use those, too).
3. IIn a medium bowl, toss the Brussels sprout quarters, halves, and loose leaves with oil and salt. Once the air fryer is preheated, transfer the Brussels into the air fryer basket. Air fry for 7 minutes.
4. IMeanwhile, prepare the aioli. In a small bowl, stir together the mayonnaise, lime zest, lime juice, garlic, chipotle powder, and salt. Set aioli aside until ready to serve.
5. IOnce the Brussels have cooked in the air fryer for 7 minutes, remove the basket and shake to stir the Brussels a little. Return the basket and air fry for another 8 minutes (15 minutes total cooking time).
6. IServe hot Brussels sprouts with the aioli for dipping.

Nutritional Value (Amount per Serving):

Calories: 102; Fat: 6.52; Carb: 8.96; Protein: 4.07

Air Fryer "Golden" Roasted Vegetables

Prep Time: 10 Minutes
Cook Time: 20 Minutes
Serves: 4

Ingredients:

- 1 lb of Yukon Gold potatoes, cubed
- 1 parsnip, peeled and cubed
- 2 carrots, peeled and cubed
- 2 to 3 tablespoon of Extra-virgin olive oil
- 1 tablespoon of fresh tarragon and chervil finely chopped
- Salt and ground black pepper to taste

Directions:

1. IPreheat an air fryer to 400 F.
2. IWash, clean and cut potatoes, parsnips and carrots.
3. IIn a deep bowl or container, combine together all ingredients and toss to combine well.
4. IPlace vegetables in an even layer in the air fryer basket.
5. IAir- fry for about 20 minutes, stirring halfway through cooking time.
6. IServe hot.

Nutritional Value (Amount per Serving):

Calories: 156; Fat: 3.3; Carb: 29.8; Protein: 3.36

Air Fryer Roasted Artichokes With Chili-Oregano Flakes

Prep Time: 10 Minutes
Cook Time: 15 Minutes
Serves: 6

Ingredients:

- 2 can (15 oz) of artichoke hearts, drained
- 3 tablespoons of olive oil
- 3 tablespoons of white wine
- 2 tablespoons dried oregano
- 3 teaspoons chili flakes or cayenne pepper to taste
- 3 cloves of garlic finely sliced
- Kosher salt and freshly ground black pepper, to taste

Directions:

1. IPreheat Air Fryer to 400 F.
2. IDrain artichokes in a colander, and pat dry on paper towels.
3. IAdd artichokes into a large container and add in all remaining ingredients; toss to combine well.
4. IPlace artichokes in Air fryer into a single layer and cook for 10-15 minutes.
5. IRepeat with any remaining artichokes.
6. IServe hot.

Nutritional Value (Amount per Serving):

Calories: 110; Fat: 7.1; Carb: 11.83; Protein: 2.8

Roasted Green Beans With Paper Parmesan

Prep Time: 10 Minutes
Cook Time: 10 Minutes
Serves: 3

Ingredients:

- 1 lb of fresh green beans, rinsed, stem ends trimmed
- Sea salt to taste
- 3 cloves of garlic, minced
- 3 tablespoon of olive oil (or garlic-infused olive oil)
- 1 tablespoon of fresh lemon juice (optional)
- Freshly cracked black pepper to taste
- ½ cup of grated Parmesan cheese

Directions:

1. IPreheat your air fryer according to manufacturer's instructions.
2. IIn a large bowl or container add green beans, and season with the salt, minced garlic, olive oil, and lemon juice.
3. IToss to combine well.
4. IPlace green beans in an even layer in the air fryer basket; cover with Parmesan cheese, and season with freshly cracked black pepper to taste.
5. IMeanwhile, spread the pine nuts out on a rimmed baking sheet and toast in the bottom third of the oven until just golden, about 5 minutes
6. ICook the green beans for about 8 minutes.
7. IServe immediately.

Nutritional Value (Amount per Serving):

Calories: 234; Fat: 18.89; Carb: 11.61; Protein: 6.94

Air-Fryer Zucchini

Prep Time: 10 Minutes
Cook Time: 10 Minutes
Serves: 2

Ingredients:

- 2 tablespoons grated Parmesan cheese
- 1 tablespoon extra-virgin olive oil
- ½ teaspoon dried oregano
- ½ teaspoon salt
- ¼ teaspoon garlic powder
- ¼ teaspoon onion powder
- ¼ teaspoon ground pepper
- ⅛ teaspoon crushed red pepper
- 2 large (8-ounce) zucchini, sliced 1/4-inch thick
- 2 teaspoons lemon juice

Directions:

1. IPreheat air fryer to 400°F for 5 minutes. Combine Parmesan, oil, oregano, salt, garlic powder, onion powder, pepper and crushed red pepper in a medium bowl. Add zucchini and toss to coat.
2. IWorking in batches if necessary, arrange the zucchini slices in a single layer in the fryer basket. Cook, flipping once, until golden brown, 10 to 12 minutes. Sprinkle with lemon juice and serve with lemon wedges.

Nutritional Value (Amount per Serving):

Calories: 58; Fat: 4.5; Carb: 2.79; Protein: 2.14

Air-Fryer Kale Chips

Prep Time: 15 Minutes
Cook Time: 15 Minutes
Serves: 2

Ingredients:

- Cooking spray
- 6 cups packed torn lacinato kale leaves (from an 8-oz. bunch)
- 1 tablespoon olive oil
- 1 ½ teaspoons reduced-sodium soy sauce
- ⅛ teaspoon salt
- ½ teaspoon white sesame seeds
- ¼ teaspoon ground cumin

Directions:

1. lCoat air-fryer basket with cooking spray.
2. lToss kale with oil, soy sauce and salt in a medium bowl; rub the leaves together well so they are completely coated.
3. lPlace the kale mixture in the prepared basket. Coat the leaves with cooking spray. Cook at 375 degrees F until crispy, 10 to 12 minutes, shaking the basket and stirring the leaves every 3 to 4 minutes. Remove from the basket and quickly sprinkle with sesame seeds and cumin.

Nutritional Value (Amount per Serving):

Calories: 253; Fat: 17.37; Carb: 22.37; Protein: 7.91

Air-Fryer Mushrooms

Prep Time: 10 Minutes
Cook Time: 30 Minutes
Serves: 4

Ingredients:

- 2 tablespoons extra-virgin olive oil
- 1 tablespoon lemon juice
- 1 tablespoon Worcestershire sauce
- ½ teaspoon onion powder
- ½ teaspoon salt
- ¼ teaspoon ground pepper
- 4 portobello mushroom caps, stems and gills removed, sliced
- 1 tablespoon chopped fresh herbs (such as flat-leaf parsley, tarragon and/or dill)

Directions:

1. IPreheat air fryer to 400°F for 5 minutes. Stir oil, lemon juice, Worcestershire, onion powder, salt and pepper together in a large bowl. Add mushroom slices and toss to coat.
2. IWorking in batches if necessary, arrange the mushroom slices in a single layer in the fryer basket. Cook, flipping once until golden brown, 15 to 17 minutes. Sprinkle with herbs before serving.

Nutritional Value (Amount per Serving):

Calories: 70; Fat: 3.72; Carb: 7.39; Protein: 4.11

Air-Fryer Beets with Feta

Prep Time: 10 Minutes
Cook Time: 20 Minutes
Serves: 4

Ingredients:

- 1 pound beets (2 large or 3 small), trimmed, peeled and cut into 1-inch pieces
- 1 tablespoon extra-virgin olive oil
- ¼ teaspoon salt
- ¼ teaspoon ground pepper
- ¼ cup crumbled feta cheese
- 1 tablespoon chopped fresh oregano

Directions:

1. IPreheat air fryer to 400°F for 5 minutes. Place beets in a large bowl and add oil, salt and pepper; toss to coat.
2. IArrange the beets in a single layer in the fryer basket; cook for 10 minutes. Carefully flip the beets and cook until crispy and browned on the edges, 6 to 8 minutes. Transfer to a serving dish and top with feta and oregano.

Nutritional Value (Amount per Serving):

Calories: 98; Fat: 3.85; Carb: 14.08; Protein: 3.57

Air Fryer Falafel

Prep Time: 10 Minutes
Cook Time: 15 Minutes
Serves: 6

Ingredients:

- 1/2 cup tahini (I like Joyva)
- 1/4 cup Greek yogurt
- 1/2 lemon, juice only
- 2 tablespoons olive oil
- 1/4 to 1/2 cup hot water
- 2 (15-ounce) cans chickpeas, rinsed and drained
- 1/4 cup fresh parsley
- 1/4 cup cilantro
- 2 cloves garlic
- 1 large shallot, chopped
- 3 tablespoons all-purpose flour
- 2 tablespoons sesame seeds
- 2 teaspoons ground cumin
- 1 teaspoon paprika
- 1/2 lemon, juice only
- 1 teaspoon salt
- Spray olive oil, for cooking
- 6 pita breads
- Fresh lettuce
- 1 large tomato, sliced thinly
- 1/2 red onion, sliced thinly
- 1 cucumber, sliced thinly

Directions:

1. IIn a medium bowl, stir together tahini, yogurt, lemon juice, and olive oil. The mixture will be very thick to start. Thin it out with hot water until it's easily spreadable. You'll have to slowly add 1/4 to 1/2 cup of hot water to get it to the right consistency.

2. IIn the bowl of a food processor, add the chickpeas, parsley, cilantro, garlic, shallot, flour, sesame seeds, cumin, paprika, lemon, and salt. Pulse until mixture comes together in a rough paste. It shouldn't be completely smooth.

3. IShape the falafel mixture into tablespoon-sized discs, about 1-inch in diameter. Repeat until you use all the falafel mixture. You should get 25 to 30 falafel discs.

4. ISpray the basket of your air fryer with some nonstick olive oil. Add as many falafel discs into the basket as you can without them touching and spray them with olive oil very lightly. Air fry the falafel at 350°F for 8 minutes. Flip and fry for another 6 minutes on the second side.

5. IRepeat until you've cooked all the falafel.

6. IServe the falafel in warm pita (I like to microwave my pita first for 15 seconds). Serve with tahini yogurt sauce and any toppings you like!

7. ILeftover falafel will store great in the fridge for 5 to 6 days, or you can freeze the falafel for longer storage. Reheat falafel in a 350°F oven for 10 to 12 minutes until warmed through.

Nutritional Value (Amount per Serving):

Calories: 404; Fat: 20.25; Carb: 45.26; Protein: 14

Air Fryer Green Beans

Prep Time: 2 Minutes
Cook Time: 10 Minutes
Serves: 2

Ingredients:

- 1 pound green beans
- 1 tablespoon olive oil
- 1/2 teaspoon garlic powder
- 1/2 teaspoon salt
- 1/2 teaspoon freshly ground black pepper
- 1 clove garlic

Directions:

1. IGather the ingredients.
2. IWash the green beans well. Trim both ends of the green beans. Keep them long or cut them into halves.
3. IToss the green beans in a bowl with the olive oil, garlic powder, salt, and pepper until they are coated in the oil and seasonings.
4. ILay the green beans in an even layer in the air fryer basket and top with the sliced garlic.
5. IAir fry the green beans at 370 F for 7 to 9 minutes. There's no need to turn them, but you can toss the basket if you wish. Serve warm.

Nutritional Value (Amount per Serving):

Calories: 129; Fat: 8.85; Carb: 10.88; Protein: 4.05

Air Fryer Chickpeas

Prep Time: 5 Minutes
Cook Time: 10 Minutes
Serves: 4-8

Ingredients:

- 1 (15-ounce) can chickpeas, drained and rinsed
- 1 tablespoon canola or vegetable oil
- 2 teaspoons fresh thyme, minced
- 1 teaspoon za'atar seasoning
- 1/2 teaspoon sea salt
- 1/4 teaspoon cracked black pepper

Directions:

1. IPreheat the air fryer to 390°F for 10 minutes:
2. IDry the chickpeas thoroughly on a paper towel or a clean kitchen towel. You can even dry them in a salad spinner, but you might lose a few depending on the design of your spinner. Discard any skins that come off of the chickpeas during this step.
3. ICombine the oil and spice mix in a bowl and whisk to combine. Gently incorporate the chickpeas until coated.
4. ITransfer to the preheated air fryer and air fry for 8 to 10 minutes until crispy. Taste one of the chickpeas; if it's not as crispy as you'd like, then continue to cook for another 1 to 3 minutes.
5. IRemove from the basket to a bowl, taste, and add more salt, pepper or seasoning to your liking. Serve immediately; the crispy chickpeas will not keep.

Nutritional Value (Amount per Serving):

Calories: 81; Fat: 3.39; Carb: 10.1; Protein: 3.03

Air Fryer Tofu

Prep Time: 8 Minutes
Cook Time: 10 Minutes
Serves: 4-6

Ingredients:

- 16 ounces extra-firm tofu
- 1/3 cup low sodium soy sauce
- 1/4 cup rice vinegar
- 1 1/2 tablespoons canola oil (or another neutral flavor oil)
- 1 tablespoon grated ginger
- 1 tablespoon brown sugar
- 2 teaspoons toasted sesame oil
- 1 1/2 teaspoons minced garlic
- 1 tablespoon sliced green onions, optional, garnish

Directions:

1. IGather the ingredients.
2. IWrap the tofu in a clean kitchen towel and place on a rimmed baking sheet. Alternatively, place the tofu on paper towels and cover with paper towels. Place a heavy skillet, a large book, or a cutting board on top of the tofu and place a few heavy cans on top to weigh everything down. This will help press excess moisture out of the tofu. Let the tofu stand for about 30 minutes.
3. IWhile the tofu stands, whisk together the soy sauce, vinegar, canola oil, ginger, brown sugar, sesame oil, and garlic in a small bowl.
4. ICut the pressed tofu into 1-inch cubes and place it in a shallow baking dish or similar nonreactive container.
5. IPour the marinade mixture over the tofu. Cover the dish and refrigerate for 30 minutes to 1 hour.
6. IPreheat the air fryer to 390 F. Arrange the marinated tofu cubes in the air fryer basket and cook for about 12 to 15 minutes, turning every 3 to 4 minutes, until crisp.
7. IServe the tofu cubes hot or cold.

Nutritional Value (Amount per Serving):

Calories: 156; Fat: 11.36; Carb: 5.02; Protein: 10.58

APPENDIX RECIPE INDEX

Printed in Great Britain
by Amazon

39309654R00064